Anthropological Lives

Anthropological Lives

An Introduction to the Profession of Anthropology

VIRGINIA R. DOMINGUEZ AND BRIGITTINE M. FRENCH

Rutgers University Press

New Brunswick, Camden, and Newark, New Jersey, and London

Library of Congress Cataloging-in-Publication Data

Names: Domínguez, Virginia R., author. | French, Brigittine M., author.
Title: Anthropological lives : an introduction to the profession of anthropology /
    Virginia R. Dominguez and Brigittine M. French.
Description: New Brunswick, New Jersey : Rutgers University Press, [2020] |
    Includes bibliographical references and index.
Identifiers: LCCN 2019033159 (print) | LCCN 2019033160 (ebook) |
    ISBN 9780813597386 (paperback) | ISBN 9780813597409 (epub)
Subjects: LCSH: Anthropology—Vocational guidance.
Classification: LCC GN41.8 .D66 2020 (print) | LCC GN41.8 (ebook) |
    DDC 301.023—dc23
LC record available at https://lccn.loc.gov/2019033159
LC ebook record available at https://lccn.loc.gov/2019033160

A British Cataloging-in-Publication record for this book is available from the British Library.

♾ The paper used in this publication meets the requirements of the American National
Standard for Information Sciences—Permanence of Paper for Printed Library Materials,
ANSI Z39.48-1992.

www.rutgersuniversitypress.org

Manufactured in the United States of America

Virginia: For the many people around the world who have chosen anthropology as a profession and for Jane Desmond's unwavering support and her commitment to anthropologists' vision, methods, and way of life

Brigittine: For my students, who continue to surprise and inspire me

Contents

Abbreviations

AAA	American Anthropological Association
ABA	Brazilian Anthropology Association
AIDS	Acquired Immune Deficiency Syndrome
BA	Bachelor of Arts
BBC	British Broadcasting Corporation
BFA	Bachelor of Fine Arts
CLIA	Clinical Laboratory Improvement Amendments of 1988
IU	Indiana University
DC	District of Columbia
DMACC	Des Moines Area Community College
EASA	European Association of Social Anthropologists
EMS	Emergency Medical Services
HIV	Human Immunodeficiency Virus
IT	Information Technology
LA	Los Angeles (California)
LGBT	Lesbian, Gay, Bisexual, and Transgender
LGBTQ	Lesbian, Gay, Bisexual, Transgender, and Queer
LLC	Limited Liability Company
MA	Massachusetts
MA	Master of Arts
MAQ	Medical Anthropology Quarterly
MD	Medical Doctor
MFA	Master of Fine Arts
MSR Lab	Microsoft Research Laboratory
NGO	Non-Governmental Organization
NIH	(United States) National Institutes of Health
PA	Physician's Assistant

Penn	University of Pennsylvania
PhD	Doctor of Philosophy
SMA	Society for Medical Anthropology
SMU	Southern Methodist University
SOS	Switch Off Something
UC Berkeley	University of California, Berkeley
UCL	University College London
UCLA	University of California, Los Angeles
UK	United Kingdom
UN	United Nations
US	United States of America
USAID	United States Agency for International Development
USSR	Union of Soviet Socialist Republics
VA	US Department of Veterans Affairs
Wash U	Washington University
WHO	World Health Organization

Meet the Anthropologists

Leslie C. Aiello

Lee D. Baker

João Biehl

Tom Boellstorff

Jacqueline Comito

Shannon Lee Dawdy

Virginia R. Dominguez

T. J. Ferguson

Brigittine M. French

Agustín Fuentes

Amy Goldenberg

Mary L. Gray

Sarah Francesca Green

Monica Heller

Douglas Hertzler

Edward Liebow

Mariano Perelman

Jeremy Arac Sabloff

Carolyn Sargent

Marilyn Strathern

Nandini Sundar

Alaka Wali

Anthropological Lives

1

Introduction

• •

The Profession of
Anthropology and What
It Means to Be an
Anthropologist

We are anthropologists. We care about making sure that people understand what we do and why. We understand that people come to anthropology in different ways, that some are students who are intrigued by a course we offer or a museum exhibit we conceive or even a field school we run in some distant place, and that others might be parents or relatives of someone who has chosen to major in anthropology or even to enter a graduate program in anthropology. We understand that some readers are potential employers faced with an interesting applicant who has majored in anthropology but is not applying for a position as an anthropologist. We understand that there are many professionals who wonder whether they should encourage or discourage young people from studying anthropology as they are trying to decide what to do "when they grow up." We understand that there are policy makers in government—at the municipal, state, or federal level—who think about and comment on the utility of anthropology (and other liberal arts degrees) for people seeking higher education. At the same time, quite often students and their families worry about their getting jobs after college, and they frequently think that the best majors are in professions they think they already understand—business, engineering, mass

1

communications, computer science. Something like anthropology may sound fascinating but impractical, especially to people who imagine the discipline to be a small profession tied exclusively to college teaching or the excavation of ancient artifacts.

We aim to demystify the discipline, to talk about what we do as anthropologists, why we do it, and what longtime members of the profession do and why they do it, in order to render the work of anthropologists more visible and understandable. Underlying these objectives is a deeply felt commitment to the utility, importance, and satisfaction of a professional anthropological life. One of the big surprises to many people—both students and others with an interest in the profession—is that in the twenty-first century over half of professional anthropologists work outside the academy. They do so in private businesses, nongovernmental organizations, and governmental agencies (Bennett et al. 2006). In these jobs, they indeed make arguments based on research, analyze situations, collect and categorize information, advocate, recommend, present materials and analyses, challenge common views, witness, testify, instruct (though often not in a classroom), consult, test, provoke, and inspire.

At the same time, those of us who have academic jobs at community colleges, four-year colleges, and research universities have a host of responsibilities and commitments in addition to our dedicated time in the classroom with students. These entail things often just briefly described as "administration" or "service"; we find those terms elusive. Indeed, they say little about this multilayered aspect of our work itself or why we do it, and it is especially ironic because that kind of work is nearly always considered an important, expected, and necessary part of our jobs at colleges and universities around the world.

What Do Anthropologists Actually Do?

This question is perhaps the most common question people outside the field ask anthropologists. Prospective majors, parents, beginning graduate students, and colleagues in other disciplines often ask us for an "inside" perspective on the professional life of anthropologists. It makes sense. People often encounter anthropology through higher education—in colleges or universities and through folks who attend them—and frequently associate anthropology with college teaching and academic research. But that only captures part of what we do, and here we seek to make the range of what anthropologists do clearer and to invite others into the practices of the profession. As the voices in this book will well illustrate, there is actually great variability in what anthropologists do in their professional lives and work.

Of course, there are some common threads in the lived practice of anthropological careers, and those are just as important to us here as showing the variety and the twists and turns of the lives of anthropologists. Consequently, we deliberately structured this book as a kind of dance in which we go back and forth between showing our commonalities as professional anthropologists and showing the great variety of what we do on a day-to-day basis in order to illustrate the range and complexity in professional anthropological lives. In different institutional locations, areas of specialization, or subfields, there is impressive diversity in our professional perspectives and actions as anthropologists. We hope that some of this range will surprise readers and will show the broad reach of anthropology in the professional world well beyond stereotypical notions of the field.

We have already mentioned perhaps the biggest surprise to most people, including entering graduate students in anthropology—namely, that more professional anthropologists work outside the realm of higher education than inside it. Like psychologists, economists, lawyers, and journalists, anthropologists work in (and for) private businesses, nongovernmental organizations, and governmental agencies (Bennett et al. 2006). They are hired for the analytic and methodological skills they acquired as anthropologists, sometimes without even realizing they were acquiring those skills until they were called on to articulate them to folks who are not anthropologists. Anthropologists can and do research almost anything that pertains to the human condition. As we have already said, they make arguments based on empirical research. They observe, listen, ask, describe, recount, question, survey, organize, and interpret. They also advocate, recommend, challenge, witness, testify, instruct, consult, test, provoke, and inspire. We mention these things again because each of these actions is central to an anthropological career and each is a skill that trained anthropologists have and often use creatively, as we will hear in the narratives of our colleagues.

At the same time, and at the risk of repeating ourselves, those of us who have academic jobs at community colleges, four-year colleges, and research universities have many responsibilities and work beyond our dedicated time in the classroom and outside it with students. We might just refer to these in passing as "administration" or "service" duties, but that kind of work is nearly always considered an important and necessary part of our jobs at colleges and universities around the world and takes up a good deal of our time.

What, then, is that work? Let us break it down a bit here to foreground some points that will appear in more detail in the chapters to follow. It entails human resource management, meaning hiring, evaluating, mentoring, promoting, and firing people. It also means faculty governance outside our own units, programs, and departments, which has an impact on large sections of our colleges and universities; evaluation of peers' research and pedagogy, including those outside our own institutions across state, national, and international borders; and assessment of academic programs, both at our own institutions and at other institutions across state, national, and international borders. It also involves leadership of professional organizations at regional, national, and international levels. Sometimes much of the work is done via committees and task forces made up of other anthropologists or other professionals from a variety of disciplines in the sciences, social sciences, and humanities. Sometimes the work is more individual, demanding a great deal of reading and assessment—of scholarly books and articles, unpublished manuscripts, and grant applications—for which there is no financial remuneration and little recognition. Sometimes the work is deliberately invisible to others, requiring the confidential assessment of other people's work and others' confidential assessments of our own work, points that we will examine in great detail in the pages to come. Sometimes the work is highly visible to others—such as leading national searches for deanships and presidencies or serving on the committees on which entire learning communities depend.

It is obvious that anthropologists do many things, much like people in certain other professions (like business and law) that are typically more visible to the general public. But this is true not just at the level of the profession as a whole but also on an individual basis in our anthropological lives. What may seem from the outside to be clear lines between responsibilities are actually blurred and traversed in the practice of our profession. For example, even the majority of anthropologists who work in business, nongovernmental, or governmental sectors report that "teaching is a primary work activity" (Brondo et al. 2009, 6). Thus, while many anthropological practitioners are not academically employed full time, they still contribute to the teaching and training of others, and they bring with them anthropological perspectives (Brondo et al. 2009). At the same time, those of us who hold teaching and research positions in academic institutions often find ourselves serving as anthropological experts for court cases in the United States (Haviland 2003; French 2015) and internationally (Briggs 2007; Blommaert 2009), testifying before Congress (Bourgois 2001), speaking on National Public Radio (Marks 2009), undertaking community assessments, and participating in commissioned scientific research panels, among myriad other roles as advocates and analysts in public life (Dominguez 2012).

This book, then, is an empirically situated firsthand examination of the *profession* of anthropology as understood through the heterogeneous perspectives offered by some leading and active practitioners. To explore the range of work anthropologists do and render it visible, we draw heavily on the sixteen written and oral interviews that Virginia R. Dominguez did while she was president of the American Anthropological Association (AAA; 2009–2011). The interviews were conducted over the phone or via Skype and were recorded at AAA headquarters, then archived and posted as an AAA series on iTunes. The whole series was called *Inside the President's Studio*. To our knowledge, faculty and students in many parts of the world listened to these oral interviews attentively and enjoyed them. To bring additional perspectives to these narratives and illustrate additional breadth in the field, we interviewed four anthropologists who had nonacademic jobs or were based outside the United States. The interviews reflect anthropological lives lived in different ways by people in many areas of anthropology, both academic and nonacademic, and these include anthropologists who see themselves as sociocultural anthropologists, linguistic anthropologists, biological anthropologists, primatologists, medical anthropologists, archaeologists, applied or practicing anthropologists, and museum anthropologists. Included in this book are perspectives generously offered by past president of AAA Monica Heller; recent past president of the Society for Medical Anthropology Carolyn Sargent; leading psychological and medical anthropologist João Biehl; archaeologist and practicing anthropologist T. J. Ferguson; noted legal and social anthropologist and journal editor Nandini Sundar; distinguished archaeologist and recent president of the Santa Fe Institute Jeremy Arac Sabloff; longtime distinguished Field Museum curator and leader Alaka Wali; well-known primatologist and past president of the Biological Anthropology Section of the AAA Agustín Fuentes; much-respected historical and social anthropologist Lee D. Baker, who is also currently dean of Trinity College at Duke University; distinguished biological anthropologist and immediate past president of the Wenner-Gren Foundation for Anthropological Research Leslie C. Aiello; widely cited and respected British social anthropologist Marilyn Strathern; folklorist and longtime (now past) editor of *Anthropology News* Amy Goldenberg; longtime applied medical anthropologist, past president of the National Society of Practicing Anthropologists, and current executive director of the AAA Edward Liebow; field-straddling historical anthropologist and archaeologist Shannon Lee Dawdy; cultural anthropologist and linguist Tom Boellstorff, who is also a recent past editor in chief of the *American Anthropologist*; British Europeanist social anthropologist Sarah Francesca Green, who is now in Helsinki, Finland, after a long and distinguished career at the University of Manchester; Jacqueline Comito, linguistic anthropologist by training and director of Iowa Learning Farms and Water Rocks programs through the Department of Agriculture at Iowa State University; Douglas Hertzler, senior policy analyst at Action Aid; Mariano Perelman, economic anthropologist at the University of Buenos Aires and the national research institute in Argentina; and Mary L. Gray, on the faculty at Indiana University and also senior researcher at Microsoft Research. We include brief biographies and lists of their most significant contributions to the field in the About the Anthropologists section of this book.

The more we thought about these interviews in conversation with our students' perennial questions and commonplace public understandings of anthropology, the more we realized that, taken as a whole, the interviews say a great deal about the range of work anthropologists do and the passions they have that are not often articulated outside the community of disciplinary practitioners to which we belong. While in the series *Inside the President's Studio* Virginia sought to introduce the world to a number of people who were part of the profession and show them as people who chose anthropology as a profession, here we want to stress what they do, why they do it, and the range of activities entailed in leading lives as anthropologists for readers who are new to considering what is entailed in the professional life and work of an anthropologist. When we quote our distinguished colleagues in this book, it is with great respect and deep interest; we also use our colleagues' voices to craft a broader analytic frame that shows how the profession looks from various positions on "the inside." In other words, we seek to render "insider knowledge" of the profession intelligible to interested outsiders and novices with the hope of encouraging further exploration, consideration, and conversation in and about our field.

We invite readers to notice the multiplicity of domains in which anthropologists work, the ways in which those change over time, and the differential skills those domains and changes necessitate. Regardless of the sector—private businesses, nongovernmental organizations, the professoriate, university administration, or museum curating—these professional experiences weave in and out of each other as one practices anthropology over the course of a career. These shifting orientations, foci, and commitments underscore that a professional life in anthropology has no unitary direction. Rather, the professional trajectories of anthropologists are multiple, converge, and often lead in new and unexpected directions. This emergent quality of anthropological work is one that allows for, and perhaps even necessitates, intellectual, methodological, and professional innovation.

Moreover, we aim to show readers that most anthropologists undertake and highlight the importance of writing as a professional endeavor, however varied the product might be. The works they produce range from the expected books and articles in peer-reviewed venues to popular books, policy briefs, legal documents, curatorial texts, and blogs. While the professional emphasis on writing remains prevalent in the careers represented here, the objectives, pleasures, and consequences of writing are always challenging and never uniform for anthropologists.

Here, then, we highlight both variety and commonality. Interviewees speak about establishing, running, and managing private and public institutions, as well as editing scholarly journals, doing research, writing, and teaching in a variety of venues, including but not limited to universities and colleges. We group a few here in order to highlight certain aspects of that work, but we urge readers to look for how these anthropologists integrate their work into their understandings of the discipline, how they describe that mix, and how what they do changes over time.

Books like this are far less common than we hope or need. Despite a growing self-conscious concern with explicating anthropological careers (Brondo and Bennett 2012), there remain few books by anthropologists that investigate the nuanced parameters of the profession. *Anthropology Put to Work*, edited by Les Field and Richard Fox (2007); Veronica Strang's (2009) *What Anthropologists Do*; and Carol Ellick and Joe Watkins's (2011) *Anthropology Graduate's Guide: From Student to a Career* are important contributions that have begun to explore some of these issues. In this era of so much talk about "the global," globalization, and planetary survival, the kind of knowledge, competence, and expertise the profession of anthropology has to offer the world seems all the more important. Yet anthropology remains a subject that is more backgrounded than foregrounded, that may be included as content in certain social studies courses young people take in high school but that is rarely named as such, unlike math, English, biology, or music. The result is that the profession looks mysterious or distant, perhaps appealing to some precisely because it is something they really only encounter in college and perhaps suspicious to others because they have had little or no exposure to it and wonder about its relevance and utility. The point of this book is to let people see what anthropologists are like, what they do for a living and why they do it, what the range of anthropological activity is, and how people approach their lives as anthropologists. We do so in order to show how, why, and in what ways careers in anthropology are productive, innovative, challenging, complicated, and rewarding.

To be clear, this book is not an introduction to the subject of anthropology. We do not seek to introduce readers to ideas, theories, or debates in the field. There are many textbooks that do that. In the United States since the early twentieth century, the standard textbook description of anthropology is that it consists of four (sub)fields in one—biological anthropology, sociocultural anthropology, linguistic anthropology, and anthropological archaeology. Textbooks usually stress that anthropology takes a holistic approach to the study of humans and argue that this differentiates anthropology from all other disciplines. Sometimes they mention that this four-field approach is not commonly found around the world, but often they fail to discuss why. There is indeed a long history of debates about how holistic anthropology really is, how students should be trained, and what happens when the four fields are not equally represented in university departments or the training of students. We do not mean to minimize the importance of those debates, but our goal here is different. We aim to show interested readers what a multiplicity of professional careers in anthropology looks like and feels like. We want to personalize the lives of anthropologists and to make them far more understandable to others who are engaged with the discipline as students, family members, mentors, employers, career counselors, and policy makers.

We think this discussion is important and useful perhaps especially because most of us do not encounter anthropology before going to college and may well come up with impressions and ideas that most anthropologists find misleading and that obscure the vibrancy of a professional life in anthropology. While *National Geographic* and the Discovery Channel sometimes feature certain kinds of anthropologists and clearly have content that aims to be serious and pedagogical (and both intersect in certain ways with the profession of anthropology), they frequently lead people outside the profession to imagine that the expeditions and activities reported there accurately reflect the work anthropologists do. Most of us do not do that kind of work. As a profession, we have people who study very affluent societies and people who study very out-of-the-way places, and in courses we teach we tend to assign articles and films made by anthropologists and published in official anthropological journals or distributed as ethnographic films. At the same time, anthropologists have long shown interest in and careful attention to all of humanity, living or dead, powerful and powerless, male and female, young and old, and all the variations within and among these categories.

In the pages that follow, we turn an anthropological eye to the lives, practices, challenges, and commitments of some contemporary anthropologists to provide a window into the profession. In chapter 2, we address anthropologists' strong recollections about how they first encountered the discipline and what about it was compelling, new, and exciting for them. Chapter 3 follows the path from an interest in anthropology to the commitment to become an anthropologist of some sort professionally. In chapter 4, we turn the lens toward an explicit focus on the many kinds of work anthropologists do, relations to the discipline and other disciplines, and institutional contexts. Chapter 5 hones in on intense professional moments and perspectives that show some of the passions, frustrations, and challenges faced by anthropologists in their work and the patterns among them that reoccur in the profession across institutional contexts. Among our colleagues' perspectives, a particular concern with public engagement emerges as a central theme. These professional anthropologists understand such engagement to be extremely important in their professional work; it sometimes brings satisfaction and other times disappointment. In chapter 6, we shift the discussion toward anthropological epistemologies and how they allow practitioners to focus on particular current or charged topics in public discourse. It examines a range of thoughts about such issues—a range that anthropologists strongly articulate and that we anchor in a disciplinary frame. We consider a few possibilities for future anthropological lives in chapter 7 and invite readers to do the same.

By way of entering into the professional lives and experiences of anthropologists, we begin by presenting some of their recollections of childhood and considering the connections between those experiences and the paths that led them to become anthropologists. We want to ground these professional lives in the experiences and subjectivities of our colleagues, and we hope that our readers find moments of both identification and curiosity.

Anthropologists in Childhood: Curiosity and Difference

That anthropology is rarely taught at the elementary or secondary school level is very unfortunate in our view. Because of the distance from the field for most people in early life, it is interesting to think of the way anthropologists grow up and how they choose to become anthropologists. In many ways, anthropologists are like most people when they are ten, twelve, or fifteen years old. In some ways, they may be a bit different, too, but it is what happens when they first formally encounter anthropology and later decide to live their lives as anthropologists that makes them anthropologists. We will take up these formative moments in depth in the following chapter. As the voices of anthropologists included in this book show, it is not some special or unusual moment in their childhood or adolescence that a parent, teacher, or employer needs to spot to ascertain how or why someone becomes an anthropologist. Rather, we will see a range of childhood experiences that create an intense curiosity about the world and a deep interest in discovering new things about it. This persistent desire that we have to habitually question often emerges with strong passions along many unexpected lines that ultimately lead to professional anthropological lives.

Some of these recollections are funny, some are poignant, and some are hard to categorize. For example, Carolyn Sargent recollected what she was like as a child. Here is what she shared with us:

> I have a photo of myself playing the piano at age two, mysteries captured me as an adolescent, and medicine intrigued me in different ways at different ages—plagues and epidemics, tales of epidemiological detection as an adolescent, colonial medicine in college, maternal and child health in the Peace Corps....
>
> When I was seventeen, I can't recall even imagining life at such an age [as now], totally ancient! Looking back, I envision several of my great aunts, with arthritic fingers, playing bridge. I think I assumed, insofar as it crossed my mind, that eventually I would morph into such a person. Now it is quite obvious that I'm never going to be a bridge player, I don't have bejeweled fingers, and refuse to have blue hair. One of my best friends is ninety-eight and in a study of the old old with remarkable cognitive capacities. She's my vision of the over-fifty set now!

Consider the words of João Biehl, who grew up in Brazil definitely not even imagining he was going to be an anthropologist one day. When asked what he was like as an adolescent, he told Virginia that at the age of seventeen he "simply loved the idea of continuing to study." Then, João said,

Studying was something quite uncommon in my working-poor background of unavailable or lost chances. I had just finished high school and had begun studying journalism and theology at two different academic institutions. In the morning I studied Greek and German, church history, philosophy, and systematic theology, and in the evening in Porto Alegre, the capital of my state, I had this intense immersion into sociology, mass communication, and writing techniques. I was quite lonely and found joy in navigating two degrees, two cities, various worlds. In the afternoon, whenever I could and had spare money, I went to see foreign films. I loved French films, the rich texture of characters. As soon as I entered university, I knew that I wanted to teach and to write books.

In contrast to this learned life, T. J. Ferguson, a distinguished archaeologist who largely works outside the academy and grew up in Hawaii, clearly had other things on his mind in high school. To Virginia's question about what he was like at the age of seventeen, T. J. replied,

I don't think I ever thought about what I would be doing thirty years later. The philosophy at the time was "Be here now"—to live in the moment. Life for me just keeps getting better and better, so thinking back to my youth now amuses me and makes me smile. As Bob Dylan sang in the sixties, I was so much older then, I'm younger than that now.

Some anthropologists, such as Jeremy Arac Sabloff, remember being "fairly studious" though also listening to a lot of early rock and roll. Others, such as Shannon Lee Dawdy, remember something very different. In fact, she matter-of-factly said that at the age of ten she "wanted to be a truck driver."

Not all anthropologists grow up being rebellious, though obviously some do. Alaka Wali described herself as a teenager like this:

I was a little bit of a rabble rouser. . . . I was a teenager kind of right after or during the time the anti–Vietnam War movement was growing and becoming prominent in 1968. I was here in Chicago as a teenager, although I don't remember [much about the 1968 events]. I did not take part of the events that were going on [but] there they were in our consciousness about social change and justice, and it was all being formed in that time and also myself having been born in India and then growing up with . . . I was affected by the racial tensions in this country, conflicts and the civil rights movement. And so all of that was a big part of my formation as a teen and trying to struggle with it.

I came to the United States when I was six years old, at the end of 1959, and there were hardly any Indian people here at the time. The immigration from India began in the mid-1960s really, and so we were kind of oddballs. . . . My father had a postdoc at Johns Hopkins University early in 1960 or 1961, I think, in Baltimore. My mother is a linguist, actually. . . . She started out in physics in India and then . . . when we moved here to Chicago she went back to school and got her PhD in linguistics. . . . They (mother and father) are both very much intellectuals of their generation. In India, at that moment when India itself was struggling against colonialism, they were the first in their families to get educated at a college or university level and then go on. So both of them represent that, my ancestral generation in that sense. And they came to this country as intellectuals really assured of [their] Indian identity. I don't think of them trying to hold on to an Indian identity. They were very cosmopolitan and, yet, you come to this country and you're immediately labeled as being people of dark skin. People don't have a way of [knowing] where to put us, and so, when we moved to Baltimore, we were always thought of as African American. . . . My parents had a lot of difficulty finding housing, and we as kids experienced what many black kids of that time were experiencing: segregation and discrimination. And so that is also part of my . . . thinking or confusion, you might say, about my identity.

Virginia pressed on a bit, asking Alaka whether she found any or all of her experiences as an immigrant to the United States ultimately helpful. Alaka's response was again very revealing about what influences a young person to become an anthropologist:

I do, in a sense, find it helpful. . . . I resent putting myself in any category. I think that is what it was [like] in my childhood—not one or the other or the third. Even claiming Indian identity didn't make sense because my parents are very atypical of what Indians were seeing here and didn't think of themselves necessarily that way. And so that, I think, has helped me as an anthropologist to be more open to experiences and understandings, as I've experienced cross-cultural or intercultural encounters in my field research.

Alaka was not alone in naming encounters with injustice as formative experiences in childhood. Tom Boellstorff describes himself as having been "nerdy and shy" as a teenager growing up in Nebraska and Oklahoma in the 1980s, a difficult time and place to be a young gay man. But not everyone we spoke with shared similar experiences. Amy Goldenberg was serious about ballet until her knees started to go out while she was in high school. Leslie C. Aiello thinks of her teen self as quite average. She was thirteen in 1959, and she describes herself as having been "a suburban California girl, spending [her] summers at the beach and listening to the likes of Elvis Presley, Frankie Avalon, the Kingston Trio, Connie Francis, Ritchie Valens, the Drifters, and Bobby Darin." To anyone who assumes that anthropologists are all rebels of some sort, her story makes us all pause and wonder. She actually told Virginia that she would like to say that she was rebellious, athletic, and intrepid, but that it just was not true. The one exception to all this, again in her own words, is that by that time she had already read the entire *Tarzan* and *Barsoom* series by Edgar Rice Burroughs, which she thinks probably foretold her future interests in anthropology and the human past.

And she is not alone among us. Edward Liebow explicitly said that he "was not much of a rebel." He was indeed a good student, actively involved in athletics and theater, and a teenager who moved easily among a number of different crowds. Ed said that his parents expected him to go to law school. Many of his closest friends in high school aspired to change the world from positions of influence, but not through research and writing.

Overall, we see that one's particular life circumstances affect one's career choices, but also how the path to becoming an anthropologist is rarely a straight line. Three extended examples are illustrative. Sarah Francesca Green, whose mother was an Egyptologist and whose father was a classicist, waxed about her childhood as a British kid largely growing up in Greece:

> Generally, my two brothers and I were seen as being different, though in what way depended on who was looking. That's probably a common experience for children who grow up outside the country to which their parents tell them they belong. Otherwise, my memories of my childhood are marked by political events: As a ten-year-old—I was living in central Athens, and it was two years before the end of the military junta under Georgios Papadopoulos. I was aware of it, and most people I knew thought it was bad. The overthrow of the junta in 1974, which centered in Athens, was the scariest thing through which I have ever lived. As a thirteen-year-old—I had arrived back in the UK the year before, when I was twelve, after ten years of living in Greece. This was the early 1970s, when there was a serious energy shortage in the UK imposed by the sudden steep rise in oil prices (I remember a three-day working week was imposed, and we were constantly exhorted to SOS, Switch Off Something). As a sixteen-year-old—in that year, I began to read academic books and was very quickly hooked.
>
> My family says I never quite grew out of having the curiosity of a two-year-old. Everything interests me and I am endlessly asking questions about things, people, situations. I also spent a lot of my childhood observing things intensely;

this was in large part because I was the youngest child of three in an extremely chatty family, and I often did not get the chance to get a word in edgewise. So I watched and listened to everything instead, and learned to notice even the tiniest details. That stood me in very good stead in later years as an ethnographer.

Like Sarah, and like Alaka, several interviewees grew up with a sense of being outsiders in certain ways. Monica Heller grew up in Montreal, but her parents were German Jews and not French Canadians. These linguistic and cultural differences were present, indeed featured, in much of her youth and led her to think a great deal about language, as she expressed in an interview with Virginia:

> I have certainly gotten sort of obsessed that most of my career has been on issues around the ways in which problems of social difference and social inequality get played out on the terrain of language. I mean that that's the sort of central thing that I keep worrying about all the time—and not just in my work but also in . . . the rest of my life. . . . Growing up in Canada, growing up in Montreal, the stuff has all been (and it still is in many respects) played out as a language issue (although it's not always clear to me that it centrally is language).

The surname Heller is not exactly one that most folks would associate with Montreal, and not surprisingly, that social fact is something that matters to Monica and strongly influenced her process of becoming an anthropologist of language. She explained,

> Well, it turns out that people in Montreal don't associate it with growing up in Montreal either. . . . We had to get trained from an early age. When people ask you, "Heller? What kind of name is that?" here's the answer you're supposed to give people: "I mean it's one of those complicated stories of Jewish migration and flight. . . . The family lore is that it was the name of an Austrian coin and so in Europe, when the Austro-Hungarian Empire, and also the Germans, decided they had to give proper family names to Jews, they sort of picked stuff and that was the one that apparently got given to my father's family. . . ."
> My father was born in Montreal [but] his family came [to Montreal] in the early part of the twentieth century before or during World War I in the classic flight from pogroms in what is now apparently the Ukraine. But my mother was a German Jew and they left Germany just before. Actually they left France in 1940. . . . Canada wasn't taking refugees at that point, but the Canadian ambassador in Paris decided he was going to disobey the government regulations and get as many people out as he could (which we found out much, much

later . . . in the 1980s). . . . Yeah, there aren't . . . many people like my mother in Montreal. [There] weren't many more people like my father [either], and I think that also sort of explains why [I have] this interest on my part. You know, Montreal is a very divided city.

I happened to be growing up at the time when francophones were mobilizing and resisting the ways in which that particular ethnolinguistic category had been used historically to legitimate class relations, and [they were saying,] "No, no, we don't have to accept being in this position any-more." Things were very explicit, very open, and sometimes quite violent. . . . And so, you know, I think [that] when you're twelve years old you ask questions about those things.

Now consider the childhood memories of Mariano Perelman, who grew up during a politically violent and economically unstable time in Argentina.

I think that my early childhood and adolescence were marked by the crises in Argentina: those surrounding President [Carlos] Menem, or what we usually just call "menemism." Those years, especially when I was fifteen, my family, like a large portion of Argentineans, went through a period of impoverishment. Even though it was not all that profound in the case of my parents, I suffered a great deal watching my father experience instability at work.

On the other hand, when I was twelve, I was sure of the importance of the Jewish religion in my way of life. This was so much the case that at thirteen I did a bar mitzvah, largely because I wanted to construct myself as a member of a large and long-lived family with a long genealogy.

From the time I was little, I was interested in reading. For example, I remember reading Agatha Christie's books as a regular and constant thing in those days. I also read [Mario] Benedetti, [Julio] Cortazar, [Gabriel] Garcia Marquez, and others. Literature was part of my life then. On the other hand, as part of developing a social life, I started going out at night and learning to drink alcohol—that is, learning bad things for sure.[1]

---

[1] Virginia has translated what Mariano wrote into English. We include his original in Spanish:

Creo que mi infancia y adolescencia estuvieron signadas por las crisis en Argentina: el menemismo. Durante esos años, en especial para mis quince años, vivimos con mi familia, como gran parte de los argentinos un proceso de empobrecimiento. Si bien no fue tan profunda en el caso de mis padres, sufrí mucho la inestabilidad con la que mi padre vivía su trabajo.

Por otro lado, a mis doce años estaba convencido de la importancia de la religión Judía como parte de mi modo de vida. Tanto así, que a los trece hice el Bar mitzvah, más que nada por mi intento de construirme en una genealogía familiar amplia y de larga data.

These are some perspectives professional anthropologists offered on their youthful selves when considering their pasts in relation to their careers. In that same spirit, we offer our own recollections and histories that inform who we are as anthropologists.

Who We Are and How We Fit In

Virginia was born in Havana, Cuba, to a pretty patriotic family of Cuban professionals, many of whom had been partly schooled in the United States even in the late nineteenth and early twentieth centuries. The family included chemists, physicists, lawyers, doctors, engineers, and accountants, nearly all of them men for many years. No one had ever studied anthropology. Architecture was deemed a good profession for a woman—especially one good in math and able to draw. But Virginia's maternal grandmother had known one of the early Cuban anthropologists, a woman named Lydia Cabrera, who, like her mentor, Fernando Ortiz, largely studied Afro-Cuban life.[2] Perhaps that helped point her in different direction.

En cuanto a mí, desde chico fue un interesado en la lectura. Recuerdo por ejemplo la lectura de los libros de Agatha Christie como una constante que acompañó aquella época. Benedetti, Cortazar, García Márquez, Arlt. La literatura fue parte de ese tiempo. Por otro lado también como parte de la sociabilidad fue el tiempo del comienzo de las salidas nocturnas, aprender a tomar alcohol, del malo por cierto.

[2] In recent years, some of Ortiz's work has been picked up by U.S. scholars in several fields, especially those interested in his concept of "transculturation." To our knowledge, Cabrera's work has not been picked up, though we certainly hope that it, too, was noticed by these same scholars. Ortiz published many books, though most were not translated into English in his lifetime. *Cuban Counterpoint: Tobacco and Sugar* appeared in 1995 in English, though it had originally been published in Spanish in 1940.

Wikipedia (2019a) mentions his year of birth (1881) and his year of death (1969) and his disenchantment with Cuban politics in the early twentieth century. It also mentions his role in the founding of several Cuban scholarly institutions and journals, including the Sociedad de Estudios Afrocubanos (Society of Afro-Cuban Studies) in 1937. It adds that "his books, *La Africania de la Musica Folklorica de Cuba* (1950) and *Los Instrumentos de la Musica Afrocubana* (1952–1955) are still regarded as key references in the study of Afro-Cuban music," and that the Cuban government established the Fernando Ortiz Foundation after his death, a foundation that sees itself as continuing his work, especially "around many cultural issues, including troubling matters like the survival of racism and racial prejudice, as well as measures that must be taken to confront these problems." It is interesting that the entry lists many of his books and mentions one of his former students (Miguel Barnet) but makes no mention of Cabrera. There is a Wikipedia entry on her, too (Wikipedia 2019b), but it fails to mention him, something that seems odd to Virginia given what her grandmother had told her. That Cabrera left Cuba in 1960, a bit over a year after Fidel Castro took over, and that Ortiz stayed in Cuba, may explain some of those odd silences and shed light on the different ideologies of the people writing their entries for Wikipedia. Her entry, for example, includes the following: "Her most important book is

When Virginia was eight, her family left Cuba and began a long process of moving to many different cities and countries. For years, Virginia's father worked for the international divisions of U.S. companies, and they periodically moved him. As the youngest of three children, Virginia stayed the longest with her parents, and by the time she was eighteen she had lived in six different societies on three continents. One might say that she was therefore destined to become an anthropologist, but she also remembers being thirteen and crying on a dark and damp winter morning in Montevideo, Uruguay, when she realized that the family had moved to Montevideo and was not just visiting. Adaptability and openness to change did not come easy but did eventually become a way of life.

That she spoke Spanish did not help much. Uruguay was quite different from Cuba in many ways, even if people in both countries spoke recognizable Spanish. Her Cuban summer was winter in Uruguay, and Christmas came in Uruguay at the start of summer. Moreover, school was in the middle of its session in July when she and her family moved to Montevideo, and she was either going to have to wait six months and lose a year of high school or learn half a year's worth of multiple subjects on her own in order to start ninth grade days after finishing eighth grade in Bergen County, New Jersey. As they were citizens of no country at the time as a result of having left Cuba after Castro took over its government and thus becoming suspect in the eyes of the Cuban government, the Dominguez family traveled with affidavits and carried both a U.S. reentry permit and a Uruguayan *titulo de viaje*.

It was only at Yale as a freshman that Virginia first encountered anthropology. She had filled out forms for Yale anticipating that her major would be sociology. This was because history and math had been her favorite subjects in high school and the handy *World Book Encyclopedia* that her parents owned once opened up to an entry on sociology, which described its concern with

---

El Monte (in Spanish, [meaning] 'The Wilderness'), which was the first major anthropological study of Afro-Cuban traditions. Published in 1954, the book became a 'bible' for Santeros who practice Santeria, a blend of Catholic teachings and native African religions that evolved among former African slaves in the Caribbean. She donated her research collection to the library of the University of Miami. . . . She was one of the first writers to recognize and make public the richness of Afro-Cuban culture. She made valuable contributions in the areas of literature, anthropology, and ethnology." Notice the absence of any mention of Ortiz or any of his works here. Her book *El Monte* describes Afro-Cuban religions, especially the Regla de Ocho (commonly known as Santeria) and the Ifá cult, both derived from traditional Yoruba religion, and Palo Monte, which originated in Central Africa. Wikipedia goes on to say, "She is credited by literary critics for having transformed Afro-Cuban oral narratives into literature . . . while anthropologists rely on her accounts of oral information collected during interviews with santeros, babalaos, or paleros, and on her descriptions of religious ceremonies."

societies and its frequent use of quantitative methods. It was really Sidney W. Mintz's skill as a lecturer and passion for his work—as an anthropologist—that made anthropology imaginable to her.[3]

For years Virginia contemplated other professions—from law to chemistry to economics, history, and foreign service—but something kept her grounded in anthropology year after year, project after project, and leadership positions in anthropology became conceivable. Every time she was tempted to move to a different profession, something about the openness and breadth of anthropology kept her from doing so. And, over the years, she has not only taught multiple anthropology courses at six universities, four in the United States and two abroad, but has also directed multiple international programs, run a national search for dean of liberal arts and sciences, served on the Executive Committee of the Faculty Senate at two U.S. universities, headed a prestigious scholarly journal in anthropology (the *American Ethnologist*), and headed the large (then twelve-thousand member) AAA. All of these roles, activities, and tasks have been part of her life as an anthropologist, guided by her training in anthropology and made imaginable by a deep immersion in, and commitment to, the profession.

In stark contrast, Brigittine grew up on a farm near a small town in Northwest Iowa, a serious student interested in other people, places, and ways of thinking about the world, with few ways to find satisfying answers. She often found many of her questions disparaged. Thus she became all too aware of the limitations and prejudices prevalent in local communities at the time in an area of the state that has elected Steve King, an outspoken white nationalist, to political office since 1996. Like many children of farmers around her, she contributed labor to the family's economic efforts, raising cattle, sheep, and pigs for the market with her father and siblings. Unlike many of them, she was troubled by the naturalized move from caring daily for young animals to selling them for slaughter, a process no one in her family or local community ever talked about openly. Silence and contradiction troubled her from an early age.

There was only one choice for college: the University of Iowa, three hundred miles away from her farm, a university that exposed her to ideas and people that

---

[3] Mintz was on the anthropology faculty at Yale when Virginia first met him. He left Yale a few years later and joined the then-new anthropology department at Johns Hopkins. He was a popular and skilled lecturer, a longtime friend and collaborator of equally distinguished Eric Wolf, a careful researcher, and author of many books and articles. Some people remember Mintz as a scholar of Puerto Rico, some as a Caribbeanist, some as the author of the highly influential *Sweetness and Power*, and some as the preeminent anthropologist of food.

fit into an anthropological life, a life that began to unfold there. To say it another way, anthropology gave Brigittine a language and a framework for building analyses of issues in the world that troubled her intellectually, emotionally, and politically. As she often tells her students, she "fell in love with anthropology" in her first class. She was compelled to immerse herself in the discipline, not knowing the specific path she would take or understanding the institutionalized process of becoming an anthropologist through a PhD program and concomitant professionalization in the field.

Brigittine's particular history and experiences of becoming an anthropologist are important to this project. Indeed, they constitute important guiding motivations for it. While Brigittine had a deep passion for the discipline from the very beginning, she had little understanding of what becoming a professional anthropologist entailed. It was Virginia who invited her into conversation about anthropology in a professional capacity. Brigittine wanted to think about the work of an anthropologist when she was a graduate student well into a PhD program. In some ways, this book is an extension of many discussions we have had together since. As a student of conflict, violence, and their discursive manifestations, Brigittine is an international teacher, researcher, administrator, and writer. Not only has she recently headed Grinnell College's Anthropology Department, but she has also served on the executive boards of the Central States Anthropological Society and the American Conference for Irish Studies. She has served as book review editor for both the *American Ethnologist* and the *Journal of Linguistic Anthropology*. She is active in interdisciplinary work on genocide, narrative, and political violence, and she remains a serious student of discourse, politics, and state making in very different parts of the world—Guatemala and Ireland.

This book is a collaboration that makes sense. Both of us are deeply immersed in the profession of anthropology, have learned its value, foster its growth and well-being, and invite others to join us from our respective and distinct positions. Both of us now have many years of experience dealing with the question so many students and their parents pose: What exactly do anthropologists do?

The chapters that follow will help answer that question and inspire readers to explore more of the range of activities of anthropology and pursue further reading and listening in our field. We turn an anthropological eye to the lives, practices, challenges, and commitments of some contemporary anthropologists. The book presents and analyzes the voices of accomplished anthropologists from across the four subfields—sociocultural anthropology, linguistic anthropology, biological anthropology, and archaeology—as well as anthropologists positioned differently in their professional roles in nongovernmental organizations, the academy, and the private sector around the world. While representing intellectual, professional, and geographical diversity within the discipline, the book serves to explicitly show the unifying threads of how anthropological knowledge is made; how it is related to the passions, commitments, and experiences of its practitioners; and how anthropologists lead their lives as engaged scholars and citizens. Through its pages, readers will gain a sense of the discipline's range of possibilities for a meaningful professional life that underscore the vibrancy, relevance, and utility of the discipline.

2

First Encounters
with Anthropology
and Its Attractions

• •

Students, colleagues in other fields, friends, acquaintances, and even family often inquire how we initially came to study anthropology and what about it was so compelling that we decided to dedicate our lives to the field. The path toward becoming an anthropologist is not an obvious one for most observers or practitioners. Despite their general distance from the field in their youth and their temporal distance from the earliest stages of their anthropological lives, when they first became seriously engaged students in the field, people who become anthropologists often remember the moment they first encountered anthropology very vividly. They remember the person who showed them a way onto an anthropological path or the precise situation in which this happened. In many of the conversations Virginia had with her interviewees and other colleagues during her American Anthropological Association presidential years, questions about how and when each person had first encountered the field of anthropology most often produced wonderful and passionate answers. Our colleagues easily recalled these moments that proved to be deeply formative and transformational experiences. They are often the kind of recollections that we tell our students and other people whom we mentor about experiencing those moments of knowing the discipline was for us; in short, discussing the aha moment when anthropology came into focus as a dedicated direction is something that many of us frequently do in the course of our professional work and over the course of our careers from students to professionals.

Often, early recollections show some of the excitement, wonder, and curiosity that spur the drive, passion, and commitment for advanced work in the field, as we will see throughout the chapters of this book. The intensity of a drive, longing, and passion for anthropology stands out as a striking feature of the perspectives represented here and, often, in the discipline more broadly. British-trained anthropologist Michael Herzfeld (2001) calls this deep desire the "siren's call" of anthropology (x). It is a notion similarly articulated by Agustín Fuentes in his reflective interview:

> I've had training in zoology, biology. A lot of that work overlaps in that area and a lot of my interests overlap in things that are on the periphery or not directly related to the mainstream of anthropology. But I am a true believer. I am an anthropological true believer. One could consider me an evangelist of anthropology. I think we have better ways at getting higher-quality answers about human becomings, human beings, and the process of the Anthropocene than almost any other discipline.

This intellectual and personal commitment to anthropology, based on a deep-seated belief that anthropology has more complicated, satisfying, and holistic answers to questions about humanity than any other field, is, in turn, connected to anthropologists' early experiences as students in some fashion. The individual transformation that one often encounters and recalls with preliminary involvement in the discipline and its practitioners underscores more broadly and collectively held values and experiences that underscore a deep commitment to the discipline and its unique perspectives (Dunn 2014). Those collectively shared understandings center around a shared passion for humanity and a deep curiosity about how best to engage the complexities of human processes, struggles, and ways of being in the world. In this sense, we do not consider it far-fetched to say that, in many ways, anthropology is a secular vocation for its practitioners in terms of depth and dedication; anthropology becomes a way of life—a way of seeing the world and a way of engaging with it. Accordingly, anthropologists often can identify a specific moment when they first felt the call to anthropology. This applies to us—Virginia and Brigittine— as well, and not just to the anthropologists we quote here or the many more we know. In that light, we think it is important to start with us.

Virginia indeed knew nothing about anthropology when she was a teenager, though she had visited a number of archaeological sites in Mexico when she was seventeen while her father was living and working in Mexico for about seven months. When Yale asked her what her major was likely going to be, she put down sociology.

She remembers having found sociology when she was a high school student in Montevideo, Uruguay. It was quite by accident. One day she just picked up a volume of the *World Book Encyclopedia* her parents had at home and it happened to open to the page that described sociology. She remembers thinking that sociology seemed to stress the social and to be largely quantitative, and she thought, "Great, history and math were my favorite subjects in high school," so sociology sounded perfect. It was not until a freshman adviser encouraged her to take a yearlong course that would introduce her to anthropology that she encountered the field and wondered if it might be a good major for her.

At the start of her junior year in college, however, she still thought she should check out sociology. She signed up for a sociology course but then dropped it in favor of an anthropology course she found more compelling. The anthropology course seemed to focus on a larger section of humanity than the sociology course. It could have been just about those specific courses, but she remembers making the switch and she remembers why. She was taking a lot of chemistry courses, language courses, math courses, and other social science courses, but somehow that sociology course did not appeal to her. The economics and political science courses she took were quite international in their orientation, and they did appeal to her. But there was something about anthropology that grabbed her in a visceral way: it dealt with the social; it was, at times, quantitative but not always; and it was largely international in its orientation and conception of humanity. When she proposed a research project under the Scholars of the House[1] umbrella at the end of her junior year, she chose an adviser who was an anthropologist. That adviser was Sidney W. Mintz. That her final exam as a Scholar of the House was conducted by an anthropologist and a sociologist made sense, but she clearly thought there was more potential in anthropology than in sociology, and it was anthropology that she chose to study in graduate school.

Coming from a rural, working-class family, Brigittine had no idea what anthropology was until she took her first class at age twenty as a sophomore in college at the University of Iowa. She recalls the pure joy she had at discovering the discipline:

> I had a general undergraduate adviser who I now realize was some kind of
> graduate student who worked with undeclared students, and he recommended
> that I take anthropology or sociology because of my interest in human social
> behavior. I resisted taking anthropology because I didn't know what it was. I
> took the sociology class instead because I recognized the subject matter of the

[1] The Scholars of the House Program existed at Yale for many years. It allowed seniors who were selected for the program to spend the entire senior year doing one project they proposed. In many cases, this involved doing research and writing a lengthy thesis. The project would be the equivalent of ten courses, and the final grade given to the project at the end of the academic year would count as the grade for ten semester courses.

discipline of sociology. I just had finished reading my father's sociology textbook over the winter break before, when he had begun studying at a community college as a nontraditional student. Well, I took the sociology class and earned an A quite easily. It was interesting, but not very challenging or satisfying. In a sense, it seemed too tidy. It was my dissatisfaction with sociology and the need to find a major that made me accept the advice to take anthropology.

The class changed my life. I immediately recognized the kinds of questions anthropologists were asking as my own questions. Their answers fascinated me and I read ahead in the anthropology textbook to learn as much as possible as quickly as possible. Within a couple of weeks, I fell in love with anthropology and quite quickly sought to declare the major because I thought that it would be full. I literally thought all of the major spots would be taken and I wouldn't have a chance to be included. I didn't know how the university worked and I assumed that everyone would naturally want to be an anthropology major!

In the professional origin narratives represented in this chapter, it becomes clear that some people were introduced to anthropology when they discovered it in college (like both Virginia and Brigittine), that others came to discover the field from knowing anthropologists within their personal networks, and that still others made their way to anthropology while looking for something they did not encounter in another discipline during the course of their formal education. As readers will see, most people first encountered anthropology while in college or at university. For some, it was through a friend or a course they happened to take. For others, it was specifically through an interest in history, historic preservation, or even an archaeological site. But we also want to point out that for all of these people, encountering anthropology affected their personal lives then and now, as well as their work paths. Each individual clearly finds that anthropology is a unique way of knowing in discernible ways; it is one that comes from the privileged position of access to higher education. Many encountered the discipline in their late teens or early twenties, but there are exceptions, too.

Sarah Francesca Green's narrative is illustrative of both commonalities and exceptions. As the daughter of a classicist and an Egyptologist, Sarah was exposed to archaeology as a child. It helped, too, that she spent much of her childhood in Greece while her father was translating classic Greek texts, so she discovered the field of anthropology much earlier than nearly everyone else included here. Sarah's experience highlights yet another common pattern. History, archaeology, and people's approaches to them caught her attention first, and then she began to reflect on them and why that was interesting and this led her in other anthropological directions.

Another noteworthy pattern is visible in our own experiences when we entered the field at different historical moments. Sometimes anthropologists, like Brigittine, grow up in small communities and wonder about lifeways in other kinds of places, and sometimes anthropologists, like Virginia, grow up moving around nationally and internationally and wonder what to make of all the similarities and differences they encounter. We know a number of anthropologists who moved around in childhood and adolescence because a parent was in the military or worked for a company that moved them around. Some experienced moments when they realized that they had just met someone or learned about a group of people who think about issues they had long cared about in ways that made sense to them. If we read these excerpts carefully, we can locate an aha moment in nearly all of them. Indeed, these are often the moments that draw students into the field to learn more and go further with the discipline. What keeps us there, in terms of a career choice, is related yet distinct and will be discussed at length in the next chapter.

In the recollections that follow, we will also see that people matter deeply to anthropologists—both with respect to individual anthropologists they encounter in the field and for people's ability to provide answers to questions they have about the social world in which we all live. We realize that people matter in other professions, too; but to read and to listen to these anthropologists talk about the draw of the discipline is to see that keen attention to people's experiences and understandings has always mattered to them in particular ways. For example, in the origin narratives of the anthropologists featured here, most are quick to note the specific professors with whom they studied, people who strongly influenced their early years in the field and who inspired them in the early moments of their engagement with anthropology. The first portion of the path into the profession sometimes merges with the paths of other anthropologists who inspire them in some way. In other instances, it is characterized by a persistent desire to understand something about people in a nuanced way. In fact, this project is born out of such ongoing reflections between Virginia and Brigittine.

By following the contours of these recollections, we may see the individual lived positions of specific anthropologists within broader intellectual disciplinary genealogies of relationships between students and professors. These embodied genealogies are not necessarily commonly visible to people within the discipline, but they are nevertheless crucial to individuals' reactions to encountering anthropology. We point out several of those people who had influential relationships with future anthropologists, examine the history of their relationships, and take care to situate them in the discipline through the notes in this chapter in order to make that "insider" knowledge more visible. All of our colleagues mentioned their mentors; some of those mentors are scholars who became internationally renowned and others less so, even as their impact on these anthropologists was equally profound.

As we uncover and follow those connections, we may begin to trace a partial outline of a history of knowledge making and mentorship unfolding in anthropology. We want to show that this happens in a way that is central to the process of encountering anthropology and, subsequently, choosing anthropological lives. It suggests a generational approach to understanding how anthropologists construct knowledge and professional lives based on what they have been given, what they have learned, and what they have been taught by the previous generation (Allen and Jobson 2016). We recognize that these relationships also may be painful and deeply problematic if and when they reproduce institutional inequalities in ways that underscore absences and harm in the process of professional training in the field (Todd 2018). In our work here, we have come to think of participating in the field of anthropology as joining an ongoing conversation that we are invited into by our trusted teachers through their relationships with us and the profession. Through these reflections with our colleagues in this book, we hope to continue and extend those conversations with our students, colleagues, consultants, and new interlocutors in and outside classrooms, conferences, and offices. We hope our readers will interrogate silences in these conversations when they find them.

In the rest of this chapter, we present a number of these first encounters grouped into small sections that highlight some of the patterns we have mentioned. We think that many of these patterns are common to most anthropologists' first encounters with anthropology and encourage more reflection on these moments among readers of this book and their own anthropological communities. These beginnings, in turn, are deeply connected to disciplinary reproduction and innovation.

Starting Out in a Different Field

João Biehl started out studying theology in Brazil but later became an anthropologist:

> As a youth I was very involved in the Lutheran community, a kind of ethnic enclave of people of German descent—I am fifth generation but still grew up speaking an oral German dialect at home—who had migrated to the urban outskirts of what was becoming a booming shoe industry hub for export in the south of Brazil. The church was a refuge of sorts from a brutal, discriminatory social and economic world. But reading the Bible was also storytelling and I greatly enjoyed teaching Sunday school, etc. The Lutheran School of Theology had strong academics with a sort of liberal arts education that was quite rare in Brazil at the time. So, very soon I learned that I enjoyed historical critical

reading and doing exegetical work, and we had a strong focus on hermeneutics and liberation theology. I was also introduced to the anthropology of religion by a wonderful Dutch anthropologist, Andre Droogers,[2] who spent several years working in Brazil before returning to the Free University.

I learned a great deal from my theological education and decided that I wanted to do a PhD in theology or social studies of religion. But before I could continue my scholarly work, I had to work in a congregation for three years. I think storytelling saved me then, too. While the church as an institution and its leaders were quite authoritarian and hypocritical, I felt that people in the congregation loved not dogmas but having their lives retold in a religious language or celebrated and mourned in rituals. At that time I also did a master's degree in philosophy and this opened the door for me to come to the U.S. and pursue a doctoral degree in social studies of religion. That's how I got to Berkeley in 1991. In sum, I did not study for the priesthood, but I was unable to find my way out of pastoral work for three years. In the meantime, I wrote two books in theology: my first book was a critical dialogue between the hermeneutics of liberation theology and feminist and black theology, and the second, my farewell to theology and the church, was called *Clandestine*. I was glad to find a different life and anthropology after this.

I love anthropology, its relentless empiricism and openness to theories and as we try to approach and name singularities and larger social processes. I remember that, when I took my first course with Paul Rabinow[3] at UC Berkeley, I had this exciting realization that I did not necessarily have to empty myself and become a vessel for a totally new set of theories and methods before I could actually begin thinking and doing anthropology. On the contrary, all that I had traversed, learned, and experienced mattered and were crucial materials to be accessed and drawn from in order to understand the present and ways of thinking and being—to be in touch with one's own demons, as [Max] Weber[4] would say, as one tries the best one can to achieve some clarity and responsibility vis-à-vis people and what is truly going on in the world.

[2] Droogers was born in 1941 in Rotterdam and became an anthropologist known for, among other things, his fieldwork in what was known as Zaire, now the Democratic Republic of Congo. His complete curriculum vita can be found at https://www.glopent .net/portal_memberdata/andredroogers.

[3] Paul Rabinow, born in 1944, is a widely recognized and widely cited U.S. anthropologist who is associated with linking the discipline with French philosophical and poststructuralist thought. See his professional website at https://anthropology.berkeley.edu/paul-m -rabinow.

[4] Max Weber (1864–1920) was a German scholar who was considered one of the great founders of the field of sociology. For years many graduate programs taught a required course in social theory that always included Weber along with Karl Marx and Emile

Then João reflected on the skills he had learned in theology and how they did and did not play out in anthropology. In talking with Virginia, he added,

> In theology I was trained to read texts closely and to excavate the contexts of their crafting and the trajectories of their meanings, and this still serves me well in the kind of anthropology I do. I am also still interested in the modern nature of religion and in its relation to social and political life. I am particularly intrigued by lay theologies, the ideas of the sacred, and the forms of human agency they convey. I am returning to these themes in a book I am writing on a messianic movement and a fratricidal war that took place among German immigrants in the 1870s in southern Brazil. When I teach medical anthropology or global health, I push students to consider the value systems underlying interventions and practices. One does not have to read theology to see that God is neither dead nor simply unconscious these days.

The path of moving from outside the discipline into it is also underscored in Tom Boellstorff's perspective. Like João, Tom was seeking something different. We could say that they were both looking for a conceptual change, something we might even call an epistemic change. Tom's perspective also highlights the importance of having a key figure introduce the novice to the field:

> I remember when, as an undergraduate, a friend of mine said, "I've decided to study anthropology," and for some strange reason I had a premonition and thought, I will do that someday. That friend of mine is still an anthropologist herself! My undergraduate majors were in music and linguistics. But for my final two years in college at Stanford, I did independent studies with Joseph Greenberg[5] and became almost a secretary to him. He was, of course, retired at that time, but he devoted incredible time to me and his work on language typology, language and thought, and other topics that influence me to this day. After a year of gay activist work after college, I entered the PhD program in linguistics at Berkeley and worked in cognitive linguistics, studying under George Lakoff[6]

Durkheim. Anthropologists often turn to Weber in contemporary times to think about foundational theories of the state, bureaucracy, and legitimate violence.

[5] Joseph Greenberg (1915–2001) was an eminent linguist who dedicated his scholarly life to investigating evidence of grammatical universals in linguistic structure. He was educated at Columbia as an undergraduate and earned a PhD at Northwestern as a student of Melville Herskovits (Wade 2001).

[6] George Lakoff, born in 1941, is a U.S. linguist who is known internationally for developing a theory of metaphor that links unconscious cognitive and grammatical structures to our habitual thought. In this way, he has brought the historical ideas of Edward Sapir and Benjamin Whorf into contemporary examination, including the relationship of metaphors to war and politics in the Global North.

and Eve Sweetser.[7] After only a year I realized it wasn't the right thing for me and left the program, working for another year for an HIV/AIDS nonprofit before entering the PhD program in anthropology at Stanford.

So my training is very odd in this way. I never really trained in linguistic anthropology; I trained in pure linguistics both as an undergraduate and for a year in graduate school. And because I never took any anthropology courses before entering graduate school, it was only while earning my PhD that I really became exposed to linguistic anthropology. I ended up coediting a book on language and sexuality, *Speaking in Queer Tongues*,[8] and writing an article published in the *Journal of Linguistic Anthropology* about gay language in Indonesia. Now, I get to teach undergraduate courses on linguistic anthropology from time to time, and teach language theory in many of my graduate courses as well. It remains important to me, and, for instance, if you look at my research on virtual worlds, you'll see I'm often attending to language and incorporating language theory. Indeed, a keystone of my new project is using theories of indexicality to rethink digital anthropology, given the origin of [the word] *digital* in *digit*, the pointing finger. It's also important to my professional sense of self in that it reminds me of the odd paths by which so many of us come to our interests and passions. I tell my story to graduate students sometimes to illustrate how you don't have to know from the outset what you will be.

These accounts by João and Tom are, of course, quite compelling, but they are not, in important ways, that unusual. First encounters with anthropology are rarely like first encounters with history, math, or literature. They typically happen later than in elementary or secondary school, and anthropologists often remember them. Consider what Nandini Sundar (who grew up in India), Carolyn Sargent (who grew up in the United States), Jacqueline Comito (who grew up in the midwestern United States), and Monica Heller (who grew up in francophone Canada) said about their first encounters with anthropology.

Like Tom, Nandini did not really begin studying anthropology until graduate school. She explained it this way:

---

[7] In addition to being a well-published linguist with a book from Cambridge University Press, Eve Sweetser (born in 1955) is also director of the Celtic Studies Program at the University of California, Berkeley. See her professional website: https://www.icsi.berkeley.edu/icsi/people/sweetser.

[8] Tom Boellstorff has been prolific in sexuality studies, linguistic anthropology, and Indonesian studies. It is interesting that he made a point in this conversation of referring to these works. *Speaking in Queer Tongues: Globalization and Gay Language* was published in 2004 by the University of Illinois Press and was coedited by fellow linguistic anthropologist and sexuality studies scholar William Leap.

I grew up in Delhi, but then I went to Oxford for my undergraduate degree and then I came to the U.S. I had done sociology in Delhi, so in a sense I always knew I wanted to do anthropology or sociology, but because I sort of had this naive idea that it's about talking to people, and I like the idea of doing that. Well, not just talking to people about themselves but just finding out about conflicts in life. So more that sort of thing. I mean I also like doing archival work and I like—I wish I knew how to number-crunch, or to analyze statistical data—so, I mean, I've always thought anthropology's exciting so I'm happy that I ended up being one.

Carolyn came to anthropology late in her undergraduate years:

Japanese, and French, and international relations [were my majors]. And then, when I was a senior in college, I took several anthropology courses, maybe as a junior and senior, I guess (but only two or three). And one of my professors, who then went on to the University of Chicago as an Asianist (an Indian specialist) said to me, "There's a grant called the Marshall Scholarship, which would allow you to go to England. I was just at the University of Manchester—that'd be great for you." So I immediately sat down and filled out the application, got a Marshall Scholarship,[9] and went without really thinking it through as well as I might have.

I went to the University of Manchester in England, where I was one of the last students of Max Gluckman.[10] It was right before he died, actually. And so I was very lucky I had one class with him. He greeted me by saying, "Ah, you're our American student. We'll try to teach you to read and write and think, but it's probably too late." Well, I called my mother and said I wanted to come home [but obviously didn't].

Jacqueline began her study of anthropology only after completing an undergraduate and a master's degree in theatre:

Once I got my undergraduate degree, I was in a program that I finished in three years. Part of the program was theater and I did theater arts. . . . And so I was

[9] Marshall Scholarships are for college graduates who are identified as "intellectually distinguished young Americans [and] their country's future leaders" (Wikipedia 2019c). They are quite prestigious and awarded for study at any university in the United Kingdom.

[10] Max Gluckman (1911–1975) was a distinguished anthropologist from South Africa who later moved to Great Britain, where he long led an impressive department at the University of Manchester. For years he tried to think about change, while largely adhering to then-dominant anthropological thinking in Britain that stressed the structure and function of human societies. He was influential in both England and Israel and is probably best known as the founder of the Manchester school of anthropology.

always in a hurry to get out of school. I loved learning and so, after I got that theater degree, I skirted around doing some theater but came back to Iowa and taught in the community college. I called myself a migrant teacher because I went from job to job traveling and had to piecemeal different things, because I got a master's degree in theater too. I got that over in England, because I really wanted to go to England. So I have two degrees already, a BFA in theater arts and an MFA or an MA in dramatic literature from the University of Essex in England.

So when I got back I could teach. I taught speech; I taught drama. I taught Comp[osition] One and I loved actually teaching speech because it brought out the best—it's kind of like teaching theater, right? Only you're doing speech, so acting. But it got old after a while going from class to class, and when you're a part-time teacher for all of those things, if you don't get enrollment, they cancel the class on you. It could even be like two days before. It was a difficult way to earn a living, but on the other hand, it was really totally free and didn't have any responsibilities.

I think I didn't even get a car until I was twenty-five and so I had the debt, my student loans, but I had no other debt, and I remember if I hadn't had [any], I used to tell my mother if I didn't [pay] my student loans, I would have been even more irresponsible than I was during my twenties. So I spent most of my twenties kind of like being almost semiretired, kind of just writing. I used to write a lot. I love to write. I was also a playwright. I wrote plays, and meanwhile I was teaching. I remember one fall, one of the classes I was supposed to teach for the spring got canceled at the last minute and I was just kind of like, "OK, screw this." I need to go back to school and get something that's going to be something a little bit more reliable for earning a living. So I pick[ed] anthropology, which is ridiculous, right? But I asked myself, "What do you like beyond theater?" and I realized that I had already been to Italy a few different times trying to learn about identity issues and all that, and when I went to Italy one time I took a book on ethology, and so I was like, I like human behavior things. I like to understand what makes people tick. So I literally looked it up in a dictionary—*human behavior*. This is before the internet. I looked it up and anthropology was mentioned, and I went, "What the hell is that?" Because I didn't have any anthropology in college. I got a BFA in theater. I mean, I had a psychology class, but I didn't have to take any anthropology. I'm not even sure Stephens College actually even offered anthropology. So I looked that up and . . . I read the description. I went, "Huh, well, that's what I like," and then I was living in Des Moines at the time and I had a job waiting tables, too, as well as teaching at DMACC [Des Moines Area Community College], so I had goals. If I was going to go back to school, I couldn't—I wouldn't—borrow money. I knew it'd be good to continue teaching to earn a living because I was not going to borrow money, but I also felt like I could get an assistantship, maybe not in the anthropology department, but at least in the speech department since I had been teaching speech. So I looked it up and Iowa State actually offered a master's in anthropology. I was like, "OK, it's close. Why not?" so I contacted Mike Whiteford[11] there and got enrolled that spring. . . . A month later I was in school. And they looked at me and said, "Well, you have no background in anthropology," so they made me take my first semester one graduate course and two of the core undergraduate courses. So I was only taking three courses there since I was still working, and I didn't have an assistantship the first semester, just basically paying for it out of pocket.

And after that I actually had an offer to teach in speech, but then the department also came up with [something] because I had so much teaching experience by that time. I had been teaching for, like, five or six years. They gave me an assistantship and Mike Whiteford (who was my adviser) and I got to work with a fabulous historian who had done Italian American work in Iowa. Her name was Dorothy Schwieder, and she has since passed away.[12] I learned how to be both a good historian and a good anthropologist, which I think are two things that actually go hand in hand.

The fact that so many anthropologists we spoke with described similar meandering paths to anthropology demonstrates the versatility and breadth of anthropologists and of the field. They also remember the challenging and generous responses of their mentors in the early days of graduate training, and here we think it worthwhile to note Carolyn Sargent's memory of her first encounter with Max Gluckman, as well as Jacqueline Comito's very different memories of Mike Whiteford.

Monica Heller, like Brigittine, is a linguistic anthropologist, but her path to anthropology was quite different. Like Brigittine and Tom Boellstorff, she arrived at anthropology through a keen interest in language and the social aspects of speech, but she was urban, Jewish, and a francophone Canadian in ways that make sense anthropologically when we hear her explain it all. She grew up in Montreal, but her family was neither anglophone nor francophone, and this presented quite a challenge for her when thinking about identity.

My father actually came home one day with a magazine of some kind—I can't remember what it was—that he found somewhere downtown with this article

---

[11] Mike Whiteford earned a PhD from the University of California, Berkeley, in 1972 and is a nationally recognized Latin Americanist and applied anthropologist.
[12] Dorothy Schwieder (1933–2014) had a long career as a historian and was the first woman to be appointed as a professor of history at Iowa State University.

about Noam Chomsky,[13] and he sort of gave it to me and he said, "Look! There's this thing called linguistics. Who knew?"

And so that's how I discovered that there was a thing called linguistics. . . . I would have majored in linguistics as an undergrad had I been able to, but it turned out that that wasn't possible. But in the sociology/anthropology department, it was possible to do language things, and there were people interested—one person interested in sociolinguistics—so that's how I discovered that there was a socio- part and that there was this whole sort of piece of it. So I sort of followed this path, you know, looking at linguistics, and [it] took me a while to sort of work through why it was that the formalist approach that dominated then (and in many ways still dominates now) in linguistics was not actually what I believe about how language works or how the world works.

The Pull of Archaeology

We found that archaeology drew both people who became professional archaeologists and people who became sociocultural anthropologists. Take T. J. Ferguson, who became an anthropological archaeologist:

I came of age in Hawaii, and went to high school and college there. My father was a career military officer, and I moved to Oahu when I was a freshman in high school. When I was a junior in college, I transferred from the main campus of the University of Hawaii in Honolulu to the Hilo College on the Big Island. During my senior year, I became interested in archaeology, and my plan was to attend the University of Arizona for professional training and then return to Polynesia. After earning a master's degree at the University of Arizona in 1976, however, I took my first job working for the Pueblo of Zuni, and it is there that I became interested in historic preservation, land claims, and cultural preservation. At Arizona, we were taught that archaeology is anthropology or it is nothing, and working for an Indian tribe enabled me to put all my anthropological training into practice. When I left Zuni, I returned to graduate school at the University of New Mexico, where I earned a master's of regional and community planning and PhD in anthropology. Then one project led to another, and I ended up staying in the Southwest, where I've been privileged to work on a series of intellectually interesting and personally rewarding anthropological projects.

[13] Noam Chomsky (born in 1928) is a well-known linguist and social activist. He is known internationally for theorizing the idea of "universal grammar" and inaugurating a new moment in linguistics known as the Chomskian Revolution. He has a parallel body of work that is quite political in which he takes up critiques of the military-industrial complex.

Jeremy Arac Sabloff also found the study of material culture compelling and became an anthropological archaeologist:

> [It occurred to me to become an archaeologist] in the fall of 1961, at the end of the semester of Anthropology 4 (Introduction to Archaeology), which was jointly taught by Loren Eiseley[14] and Froehlich Rainey[15] with many guest lectures by curators from the University of Pennsylvania Museum in my sophomore year at the University of Pennsylvania. I didn't collect arrowheads or have [an] interest in pointed facts, but when I went to college [I'd] never even heard of archaeology. It wasn't on my radar screen in the slightest, and literally it wasn't until my sophomore year at the University of Pennsylvania when I went [and] we were randomly assigned advisers. [He] said, "What are you going to major in?" And I think I said something like, "I don't have a clue," and he said, "You know this is the beginning of your sophomore year. It's not too early to begin thinking about that." But he was actually very good. So he drew me [in] and said, "What are your interests?" And I was interested in aspects of history and architecture, and he said, "Have you ever been down to the university museum?" and I said, "No." And he said, "That's probably the best department in Arts and Sciences at Penn right now, the Anthropology Department." And I don't think that I stupidly asked, "What is that?" but it was something kind of close. He said, "Why don't you go down to the university museum and take a course in archaeology?" And I said yes. I was just fortunate enough that the introduction to archaeology was jointly [taught] by Loren Eiseley and Froehlich Rainey, who was director of the museum [at the time]. And they brought in a host of curators of the museum across the board [to] give guest lectures and so on. I was just very taken by the nature of archaeology and the interest [they had], be [it] Samuel Kramer[16] talking about Sumerian writing [or] Beth Ralph[17] talking about new breakthroughs in

[14] Loren Eiseley (1907–1977) earned his PhD at the University of Pennsylvania and taught there for several decades. He was an anthropologist who achieved wide acclaim more broadly as a natural science writer.

[15] Froehlich Rainey (1907–1992) was an U.S. archaeologist who worked in Alaska for the U.S. government during World War II. In addition to a prolific academic career, he hosted a popular television quiz show called *What in the World?* about archaeological and natural scientific facts that ran for fifteen years. See https://www.youtube.com/playlist?list=PL56C1C55B10899C57.

[16] Samuel Kramer (1897–1990) was an immigrant to the United States from the greater Russian empire, where the family had faced anti-Semitism. As a youth, he studied Hebrew extensively and became an internationally recognized expert on Sumerian language and culture. See Kramer (1988).

[17] Elizabeth K. Ralph (1921–1993) was a pioneer in the technique of radiocarbon dating. She earned graduate degrees in physics and geology and founded the C-14 lab at the University of Pennsylvania (Archeological Institute of America, n.d.).

radiocarbon dating in the museum lab. . . . It was the broad ideas. I became aware of many of the difficulties that a field archaeologist faced during my first summer fieldwork in 1963, when I was a crew member on a team that was part of the River Basin Surveys in South Dakota and Nebraska, but I also had my intellectual excitement about archaeology reinforced by the enjoyment of fieldwork.

Archaeology also initially entices many students to the field of anthropology, even when they ultimately find their way to sociocultural or linguistic anthropology. Perhaps it is because there is more media attention to it, and perhaps it is because young people often want to visit archaeological sites. Whatever the reason, many first encounters are with anthropological archaeology.

Consider Marilyn Strathern's discussion of how she first encountered anthropology. She is one of those distinguished anthropologists who became a social anthropologist in England but who encountered social anthropology after she encountered anthropological archaeology. Here we quote her describing her experience:

> I can't think of a time when I didn't know about social anthropology, but it must have been in my late teens at school. I used to go digging (Roman remains), loved archaeology, but was also inspired by my history teacher at school (we did the eighteenth century and I read a bit of Rousseau and had grandiose ideas about the study of society). I found the combination of archaeology and anthropology in the first [undergraduate] year at Cambridge irresistible. If I hadn't gone to Cambridge, I would have gone to Oxford and read history. I was bowled over by two books before really starting the course: *Structure and Function*[18] completely fascinated me; the description of the cattle bells in *The Nuer*[19] gripped me for its detail and evocation.
>
> I would include my parents among my teachers—e.g., my mother was teaching adult education courses on women and art, women and literature, etc., before second-wave feminism began. I have no idea what she thought. Our companionship was taken for granted perhaps and she must have found me receptive, possibly overstudious, but also lazy. I do recall her lamenting (for not trying to train it) my atrocious memory (something that has been atrocious

[18] *Structure and Function in Primitive Society* (1952) was a much-studied book by one of the leading figures in British anthropology, A. R. Radcliffe-Brown (1881–1955). He mobilized tenets of Durkheimian ideas in developing his theory of structural-functionalism, a theory that became a guiding orientation in anthropological analyses on both sides of the Atlantic during the interwar years.

[19] *The Nuer* (1940) was another much-studied book by an equally influential and important figure in British anthropology, E. E. Evans-Pritchard (1902–1973). He also applied structural-functionalist theory in much of his work and certainly in this book.

ever since), and I had none of her language skills. My university teachers? Did they think I was shy, clever, not speaking up enough? I had intellectual confidence, not social confidence. Significant university teachers included Meyer Fortes[20] and Edmund Leach[21] (via their undergraduate lectures). They were inspiring. Individual supervisors over the three years as an undergraduate: they were mediators between me and the discipline. I didn't really stop to think what I thought of them, though I became fond of all three.

Sarah Francesca Green, who also became a social anthropologist in England, before moving to Finland, recounts a somewhat similar trajectory:

I knew about the existence of anthropology from a young age, because my mother had studied some anthropology at university (she later became an Egyptologist). My decision to become an anthropologist was made more than once. The first was when, as an undergraduate studying both archaeology and anthropology, I shifted my attention more to anthropology. The second was after my former director of studies at university persuaded me to apply for a scholarship to study for a PhD. That was a major decision. Third, after completing the doctorate, I applied for a job as a postdoctoral research fellow and was awarded it. And finally, I applied for a permanent job at Manchester and was appointed to a junior post in 1995. It was at that moment, I think, that I decided that perhaps my past in journalism and law, in both of which I dabbled after I graduated, were over.

Yes, when I first went to university, my idea was that I should become an archaeologist. In Greece, I was surrounded by material evidence of all the stories my father told about the classical Greeks, which also brought alive his stories about the Romans, and my mother added to that with her knowledge of the Egyptians.

However, once I got to university, I realized that my experience in Greece had highlighted the politically charged complexity of the relationship between the past and the present. I was aware that all the classicists I knew in Greece were, like my father, not Greeks, but scholars from other countries. It seemed to me there was something interesting going on there about how Greek

[20] Meyer Fortes (1906–1983) was a South African national who became one of the major figures in British structural-functionalist thought. He did extensive fieldwork and writing on West African kinship, politics, and religion. His research influenced the theoretical development of the Manchester school of thought.
[21] Sir Edmund Leach (1910–1989) was also a major figure in British social anthropology. He initially spent his postcollege life working for business interests in China and then enrolled in graduate school in England. His body of research is most known for his ethnographic and theoretical analyses of highland Burmese hill tribes, his impact on political anthropology, and his writing on Claude Levi-Strauss's structuralism.

classical history had been written. Whatever it was about, it was not closely related to contemporary Greece; that just happened to be where the archaeological sites were located. So as I began to learn more about social anthropology through university, I came to the conclusion that this was where my deepest interests lay, and that this discipline could provide me with a means to think about those kinds of issues.

The Aha Moment

Many anthropologists we interviewed recalled their personal aha moment. Notice that for all of them, their encounters with anthropology, in one way or another, affected them deeply. For Agustín Fuentes, anthropology satisfied longtime interests and yearnings:

> I always was interested in what makes humans tick, in travel, in human variation of all stripes, and in the world of animals and humans' place in it, but I did not really connect this with anthropology until my second and third years of undergraduate studies, where I had courses with Phyllis Dolhinow,[22] Laura Nader,[23] and Andrei Simic,[24] who was visiting at UC Berkeley then, and it was at that point that I realized anthropology existed and that it was more or less what I was looking for. I was a nineteen-year-old sitting in a primate behavior class and Phyllis Dolhinow, who later became my graduate adviser, was lecturing about chimpanzees and langurs, and she referred to individuals as she proceeded to describe a day in the life of these individuals, and I was hooked.

Edward Liebow, the current executive director of the American Anthropological Association and a longtime practicing anthropologist for Battelle in Seattle, said he was hooked right from his introduction to anthropology:

[22] Phyllis Dolhinow was born in 1933 in Elgin, Illinois. She earned a PhD from the University of Chicago and is the author, coauthor, editor, or coeditor of several books in biological anthropology.

[23] Laura Nader was born in 1930 and is a prolific social and legal anthropologist who has been on the faculty of the Anthropology Department at the University of California, Berkeley, for over forty years. She is author or coauthor of multiple books; lead, director, or producer of three films; and author or coauthor of hundreds of articles on a range of topics, including law and alternative dispute resolution. She is a visionary thinker who has called for anthropologists to "study up"—to examine those who produce and wield power in culturally specific contexts. Her brother is former U.S. presidential candidate Ralph Nader.

[24] Andrei Simic (1930–2017) became a professor of anthropology at the University of Southern California.

First term as an undergraduate, I took an introductory seminar from Paul Riesman,[25] and I was hooked. He was a new prof, had just finished his dissertation from the Sorbonne and had it published as *Freedom in Fulani Social Life*. He had written this manuscript, in French, exploring the concept of freedom and the relationship between the individual and society among a group of pastoralists of Burkina Faso. I had never been exposed to such careful, thoughtful discussion; we read ten autobiographies in ten weeks, all chosen from different settings. I loved the vocabulary, the problem sets, the alternative points of view.

Anthropology allowed Amy Goldenberg, who became a folklorist, to delve into her overlapping interests in the Soviet Union, dance, language, and politics, which were first ignited in childhood. She said,

By the time I started college, I was very interested in language and culture, especially Russian. I [had taken] a lot of ballet growing up, and it was obvious to me that all the best dancers in the U.S. had defected from the Soviet Union. At the same time, in the early eighties, a lot of my classmates at school would echo whatever Soviet stereotypes were popular then and talk about evil commies. But I was intrigued by the USSR. I was convinced there was something interesting going on over there because they produced the world's best dancers. Of course, it was also obvious that negative stuff was happening too, since so many of them had in fact defected.

So I signed up to study Russian as soon as I could. The department also offered a series of Russian folklore classes. I didn't really know what it was, but the course descriptions spoke directly to my interest in culture. I signed up and loved the class. Plus the teacher was inspirational. So I signed up for the next one. One afternoon after that class, something clicked, and it seemed everything in the world could be explained through folklore. Then I took some classes with another folklorist who was in the Anthropology and English Departments. I found out that the subject was fascinating no matter what culture or region we were discussing, and I just kept on going with it....

I spent a year in Russia after graduating from college. After that year, I spent a few weeks traveling in Eastern Europe, including Poland. Later, when I was thinking about future research and fieldwork, I just kept on thinking about Poland and the possibilities. So I made the plan to revolve around work there.

For Alaka Wali, who became a cultural anthropologist and a museum curator at the Field Museum in Chicago, anthropology broadened the perspectives

---

[25] Paul Riesman (1938–1988) was a long-standing member of the Anthropology Department at Carleton College and author of *Freedom in Fulani Social Life* (1977).

she already held about social justice and tied together seemingly disparate struggles. In this she is both typical and unusual among anthropologists. She said,

> In the 1970s, I had the opportunity to go to Chiapas as part of the Harvard Chiapas Project.[26] And that really is where I came to fall in love with working in Central and South America. And also at that time Shelton Davis,[27] [also known as] Sandy Davis, was teaching at Harvard and bringing to the floor these issues about Indigenous people in Central America, the Amazon, and North America. And so we were hearing about what was happening to Indigenous people at the same time that we were protesting the Vietnam War. We started, as undergraduate students, to begin to take up the cause of Indigenous people, and so I became part of that group that started working with Indigenous people in Central and South America.

Leslie C. Aiello, who became a distinguished biological anthropologist, lived and worked in England, and is now the immediate past president of the Wenner-Gren Foundation for Anthropological Research, describes being piqued by several of anthropology's subfields:

> I first encountered anthropology as a freshman at UCLA. A combination of a great introductory class (Wendell Oswalt)[28] and an eight-week archaeological field school in Cedar City, Utah, convinced me to change my major from zoology/geology to anthropology. I hate to admit it now, but I remember sitting in a lecture and thinking that since I was a woman, I wouldn't have to worry about supporting myself and could study what I really enjoyed. This was in 1963 and the world was different then.
>
> The 1960s was a great time at UCLA and there was a strong faculty across the subdisciplines. By the time I began graduate school in 1967, I was a committed Upper Paleolithic archaeologist. I was introduced to feminism by

---

[26] The Harvard Chiapas Project was a research project led by Harvard professor Evon Vogt for decades. It aimed to teach students how to do ethnographic fieldwork just as much as learning about the languages, cultures, peoples, and history of the area itself. It began in 1957 and trained several leading Mayanists as well as other anthropologists of Mexico over generations. It ended in 1980.

[27] Shelton Davis (1942–2010) was a U.S. sociocultural anthropologist known for his contributions to Latin American anthropology and Guatemalan ethnography and his concern for Indigenous rights in the region.

[28] Wendell Oswalt was born in the United States in 1927, joined the coast guard during World War II, and earned a PhD in anthropology from the University of Arizona. His website (Oswalt, n.d.) discusses at length the highlights of his professional and personal life while articulating his vision for, and approach to, anthropology.

Sally Binford[29] (who was a friend and mentor throughout this period), and I had been introduced to fieldwork in the South of France by Jim Sackett,[30] and to human evolution by Bernard Campbell.[31] It was a very exciting period, particularly in the context of the social and political atmosphere of the time.

Lee D. Baker, who became a historical and cultural anthropologist and university administrator in more recent years, also arrived at anthropology in his search for answers to questions about the racism and oppression he encountered both in the United States and abroad. Notice how important this was to him as he recounts his first encounters with anthropology in his interview with Virginia:

In high school I did an exchange to Australia. It was called American Friends Services, and I lived with an aboriginal family in the outback of Broome, Western Australia. I thought I was going to be hanging out in Sydney and surfing, but I was placed in this . . . very affluent and educated aboriginal family that provided medical services to people in the missions, so people who were not in the city but in the tribal areas would have access. And so looking at all the contradictions and grappling with my own identity—with race and racism—I saw for the first time that Aboriginals are treated a lot like African Americans and Native Americans. This was at the height of the crack epidemic, and I was really sensitive to people losing their families and losing their houses because of crack. But the aboriginals were sniffing petrol and getting drunk. I was like, "What the hell is going on?" because they are both black [but live] in white societies. Is this just race? I was only seventeen years old. I didn't have any answers to these things, and so then to answer those questions I initially had in high school, I thought, "Well, anthropology will help me. If I study African American studies and anthropology, I will be able to help explain or help myself understand what is happening in Australia." And so that is how I applied Anthropology 101 my freshman year. In the fall in my freshman year, . . . I declared my major when I walked in the door.

---

[29] Sally Binford (1924–1994) was a talented Old World archaeologist and, later in life, a publicly engaged feminist. She, along with her then husband, Lewis Binford, were leaders in the development of the theoretical shift to processual archaeology. She left the academy formally but was actively involved in second-wave feminism and embodied its tenets in her life choices. See Wragg Sykes (n.d.).

[30] James Sackett earned a PhD from Harvard in 1965. He is an Old World archaeologist on the faculty at the University of California, Los Angeles.

[31] Bernard Campbell was born in England in 1930 and is an Old World archaeologist. He is the author of a popular textbook (Campbell 1966) that is now in its sixth edition. See InformIT (n.d.).

Later I was taking a class at Portland State in black studies and we were studying the Harlem Renaissance and, at the same time, I was taking a theory of anthropology class and going over the important work Franz Boas was doing in improving race relations. My hunch, at the time, was that Boas was at Columbia University, basically in Harlem, and that he was not doing this all by himself. I pushed my professor, Dan Scheans,[32] at the time, and he told me to figure it out. I guess I am still pursuing questions I had as an undergraduate.

It becomes clear in talking to anthropologists that many found their initial motivation to formally join the discipline out of a concern with inequality and social justice. Douglas Hertzler, who started his professional career teaching and administering international internships for students and now works as a policy analyst for an international nongovernmental organization, told Brigittine,

I had just come back from three years of volunteering in Bolivia. And so I was in a very rural area, a long ways from any city, in the forest—on the edge of the area which was being deforested as, sort of, agriculture was advancing into that area, and I saw a lot about the social organization of the mostly Quechua-speaking peoples that were settling in that area. And they were in a new place. Some of them had been there ten years but they were—it was a new environment for them and the social organization was very interesting to me. The conflicts and struggles with large local landowners and other issues were interesting, and I was just trying to make sense of this whole displacement of people and what was happening and the social struggles and what it meant to have social justice or for people to have equality. And, of course, Bolivia was a very different place. This was 1991 when I returned from Bolivia. I first went there in 1988 and it was a very different place than it is now in terms of Indigenous peoples' empowerment. But so as I was trying to—you know there was a lot I didn't understand even after three years of living and working on—I was working on agroforestry projects mostly but a whole range of agricultural and community development projects—everything from water wells to some different crops and trying to figure out what kind of farming system would be sustainable in this area, along with local community organizations. And it was actually—when I sat down to read this, I read two different books by anthropologists, and I'll just say the one that was really helpful to me—there were two. One work analyzed, sort of, the two major ethnic groups, if you will, of that—or identities of that particular region of the country in eastern Bolivia.

[32] Daniel Scheans (1929–1995) was a sociocultural anthropologist who was on the faculty of Portland State in the Anthropology Department from 1965 to 1989. There is a scholarship in his memory for current students there.

There were, you know, Cambas and Cholas, and Chola was a pejorative term used by the lowlanders and the term Camba was actually a pejorative term as well for lowlanders used by the upper class but then sort of rapidly adopted by them, to understand this sort of clash with this migration of people coming from the Bolivian highlands.

But that book—you know, that work by that anthropologist did not explain it as well to me as did as another book, which was based on the dissertation. It was by Lesley Gill [1987], who's currently at Vanderbilt. But she wrote a book based on her doctoral dissertation which really helped me understand the whole political economy of the region. So, you had, you know, those two works but it was really Lesley Gill's work which looked at the political economy of agriculture in eastern Bolivia that drew me to anthropology to understand more. And so I began thinking about going to graduate school in anthropology as a result of reading that in that period after I returned. And I went back—I applied to graduate school and went back to Bolivia for about ten more months and then came back and started at the University of Iowa.

Reflections on First Encounters with Anthropology

Overall, those of us who are drawn to acquiring that distinct and privileged "professional anthropological vision" (Goodwin 1994) of the world that anthropology offers often recognize a particular value in the ways that anthropology helps to denaturalize familiar and taken-for-granted ideas about the way the world works and humans' place in it. This anthropological "critique of common sense" (Herzfeld 2001) allows questioning people to interrogate deeply the assumptions that humans have about each other across time and space. This critical orientation unfolds across the subfields in a fundamental and enduring way and is coupled with either the intimacy or the breadth of an anthropological perspective, inspiring deep passion among anthropological practitioners, as each of the twenty-two colleagues' narratives appearing in this book clearly attests. It does not seem to make a huge difference in the next steps someone takes to become a professional anthropologist if that person first encountered anthropology through an anthropologist who inspired him or her or if that person first encountered anthropology while asking certain pressing questions in the midst of other fields. What matters is that there was always a first encounter that was striking, that felt right, and that eventually became a way of life.

Topics of interest have varied, of course, but something about the field's approach to the world and its broad interrogation of issues such as sameness and difference and continuity and change struck a chord with each one of us when we first encountered anthropology and encouraged us to eventually choose to become anthropologists. For some it was "human existence" in its historical and social context. For some it was the massive variety of the human experience on the planet. For some it was those material remains of past human civilizations that called out to us, making us wonder what those lives were like and why those societies are no longer with us. For some it was realizing that the public's general sense of a place or a people was often misguided, too wrong, unfair, or simple. For others, it was the openness to any topic pertaining to humans and the commitment to fighting stereotypes and other forms of social injustice from an empirical perspective—a "relentless empiricism," as João Biehl said. And it led to myriad paths—to studying health and reproduction, Indigenous lives in the present and the past, societies and languages often ignored by others, contradictions in other people's lives as well as our own, and institutions of learning that many people trust and others don't.

Whether we came to the field from another discipline or arrived at it with burning questions that came to us from our own life experience, many of us have had the happy realization that João described when he said, "All that I had traversed, learned, and experienced mattered and were crucial materials to be accessed and drawn from." The field allows intellectual range, encourages openness to difference, and promotes a combination of passion and objectivity in our thinking and our work. In one form or another, each one of us has found that mix profoundly appealing in ways that allowed us to flourish in our chosen work lives.

It is revealing that most of us did experience a particular moment of exposure to anthropology, that aha moment, or meet a person who led us to anthropology. Like some other fields, anthropology is typically not something we encounter in secondary school; rather, it is a field that most of us encounter in the context of working with colleagues, studying with colleagues, or otherwise having relationships with people in higher education. It suggests that it is important to further consider how anthropological approaches are or are not valued in public education and how we gain access to these formative experiences. When we do, encountering anthropology is a very formative experience and it frequently elicits deep commitments and enduring passions that last a lifetime. This central theme of passion is something we have chosen to highlight in chapter 5 by looking at the enduring and deep commitments each one of the anthropologists we include here brings to her or his work and professional life.

3

Anthropology as a Choice
and a Profession

●●●●●●●●●●●●●●●●●●●●●●●

We have already talked about how these twenty-two anthropologists first encountered anthropology and what kinds of jobs they have, whether it was exactly what they were trained for or not. Now we want to follow their paths to focus on their choice to become anthropologists and not professionals of a different sort, when they made those choices, how those choices relate to those of people in other fields, and how anthropologists interact with people in other fields. We present in this chapter the way these anthropologists talk about the moves they made from encountering the discipline as a unique field to joining the profession, two distinct moments in the course of anthropological lives.

We begin with our own trajectories. As Virginia said before, she was not thinking of anthropology as a profession in high school at all. It was not until her senior year in college, when she was applying to graduate schools, that she considered it seriously as a profession. Throughout college she took many courses in other fields—from chemistry to economics and Russian. But after doing a lengthy bit of fieldwork in New York City under the guidance of eminent anthropologist Sidney W. Mintz, she applied to several doctoral programs in anthropology (in addition to a professional MA program at the Fletcher School of Law and Diplomacy at Tufts University). She thinks that anthropology's differences from other fields (but also connections to other fields) made the choice clearer in her mind, but it could also have been simply working closely with Mintz during her senior year in college and wanting to do work much like what he did. Virginia had been exposed to a number of other fields, and she had especially contemplated law, but anthropology appealed to her more because it seemed to require more thought and more research than law, and the fact that all of humanity mattered to anthropology sealed the deal.

As Virginia looks back on her own trajectory, it makes sense that she has come to have close working connections with colleagues in American studies, history, religion, political science, law, and communication studies, and that she has even published jointly with colleagues in some of those fields. She partly works on the United States and partly outside the United States (especially Israel), and her methods include archival work, work on institutions that legal scholars and political scientists tend to do, and visual work (including films) that communications studies scholars do. But anthropology is definitely home base (like it was for Mintz), and that identification has made her think of herself not just as an anthropologist but also as an advocate for anthropology in many different settings nationally and internationally.

Why, one may ask? We have already talked about how anthropology is rarely taught before college. This means that many people do not know about it, unless they happen to come across it earlier, and this bothers Virginia because she has found it to be very worthwhile and she wants others to see its value, too. Her own trajectory has led her to see that anthropology is less well known in many countries than history, literature, math, or engineering and that this means that it needs people to advocate for its usefulness and value as members of the profession.

Although Brigittine has studied anthropology her whole adult life, she remembers very clearly when she first identified anthropology as her profession. She was on a return flight from Guatemala after completing the last phase of her formal doctoral research. The flight attendant handed out the immigration boarding cards for inbound U.S. flights. She was confronted with the occupation line, and where she had always put "student" during her many field trips to Guatemala in the several years before, she now wrote "anthropologist." It was a key moment when she claimed the profession and her new and tentative place in it for the first time. Soon after that, while she was writing her dissertation, one of her graduate school mentors, Nora England,[1] told her that earning the PhD was the beginning of a professional career, not the end. Those words resonated with her perhaps more than Nora knew at the time; it was an

---

[1] Nora C. England (born 1946) is an anthropological linguist who has devoted her life to the analysis of the grammatical structures of Mayan languages and the empowerment of Maya and other Indigenous peoples in the Americas. She won a MacArthur Fellowship (the "genius grant") in 1993, founded Oxlajuuj Keej Maya' Ajtz'iib' (a nongovernmental organization of Maya linguists), and is the founding director of the Center for the Indigenous Languages of Latin America at the University of Texas in Austin.

inside perspective offered by a senior scholar, a confirmation of the openness of the path to follow, and a challenge to make a career that was meaningful. For Brigittine, it was both an exciting and uncertain moment.

Each of the anthropologists we interviewed chose anthropology as a profession in a deliberate and conscious way in at least two moments, perhaps more. In so doing, each chose to make the commitment to be trained in anthropology at the doctoral level and then to work as an anthropologist after completing the degree. Sometimes they also actively considered other fields or professions before choosing anthropology for personal, familial, experiential, and intellectual reasons. The reasons varied somewhat—and we want to mention those variations here—but they also were pretty consistent and coincide well with the enduring passions we will discuss in the next chapters. Briefly, we consistently see that the choice of a professional anthropological life is linked with deeply held understandings of, and commitments to, the world. These understandings and commitments are central to most anthropologists, regardless of their generation or the language in which they speak or write. They may speak about social justice, study family patterns and poverty, teach about ethnocentrism and xenophobia, or worry about the position of women, but it is the fact that anthropology cares about all of humanity and not just those in cities or in prosperous countries that compels them to do so.

Carolyn Sargent is a great example of someone who chose anthropology while immersed in other jobs and serious hobbies. She was in the Peace Corps in West Africa after college and before she committed to training in anthropology. She found that most of her work as a Peace Corps volunteer concerned health issues, women's health, and health delivery systems, and yet she chose anthropology—with gender and medical anthropology as her foci—rather than go to medical school, physician assistant school, or even nursing school. She has also long been a gifted pianist, but she chose to study anthropology and not attend a conservatory or even earn a degree in music. How she has managed all these interests and talents is a good illustration of choices anthropologists make over the course of their lives.

Monica Heller's path provides yet another great example of the process of choosing anthropology over other likely professions. As we learned in chapter 2, she grew up in Montreal aware of many serious linguistic issues in Canada, and specifically francophone Canada, but she chose anthropology—linguistic anthropology in particular—over linguistics, literature, or political science. Why she made that choice, and eventually became president of the American Anthropological Association (AAA), is worth contemplating here. It was clearly an active choice that required a great deal of commitment and vision. Language issues can be explored in a variety of different professions, and yet she made anthropology her profession. Language matters a lot to Monica, but it became clear to her over the years that language was best studied socially, politically, and contextually, and that it was best to do so with the tools of anthropology.

T. J. Ferguson grew up in Hawaii, very much a product of his time and place, and chose to become an archaeologist in the context of anthropology. He also chose to work mostly outside academia, setting up a business of his own and largely working with Native American communities to do archaeological work they want done and advocate for them, when that is necessary. He could have chosen many other careers, including a number of other types of archaeology, from classical archaeology focusing on ancient Rome or ancient Greece to biblical archaeology, but he did not. T. J. became an anthropological archaeologist in a very conscious and deliberate way. This meant working with Indigenous communities, always checking to see what they wanted done, and being concerned with the politics and ethics of his own work.

Tom Boellstorff, recent past editor in chief of *American Anthropologist*, the flagship journal of the AAA, could easily have become an actor or a musician, both of which he was impressive at in high school and college. As discussed in earlier chapters, Tom grew up in Nebraska and Oklahoma because his father was a geologist and had jobs there. They were urban but surrounded by farmers in both states. And yet neither geology nor agriculture captured Tom's imagination. He was seriously into drama and music through his teens and even majored in music at Stanford. But linguistics made sense to him, cultural anthropology made sense to him, and activist work with gay communities in and outside the United States made great sense to him. That anthropology provided a professional space that allowed him to pursue all of these interests at the same time clinched the deal for him.

Virginia frequently asked the people she interviewed if they had ever considered public office—running for president (of the United States), getting involved in electoral politics, or getting into diplomatic work. This was a way of asking if they had ever considered other professions, if they saw anthropology influencing public policy, and if they thought about themselves engaging with the wider public, even leading it. Few said they had considered it; instead, many indicated that they had come to anthropology very deliberately and with the idea that it would allow them the greatest freedom to choose topics, approaches, concerns, and paths to which they could dedicate themselves over time. Many of those interviewed have ranged in areas of expertise, succeeded as leaders at various levels of the anthropological profession, and done what many of us call engaged anthropology—activist work, advocacy work, and policy-oriented work in which we make academic knowledge explicitly articulate with different aspects of the public—as we will discuss at length in the following chapter. It is mostly outside the United States that anthropologists, such as Miguel Vale de Almeida in Lisbon, Portugal, or Ashraf Ghani in Kabul, Afghanistan, have held electoral office.[2]

This two-pronged approach of conducting some form of research and participating in some form of public engagement, however broadly construed, may be the hallmark of these and many established anthropologists, but it is clearly also the preference of many younger anthropologists, particularly those interested in joining the profession today. One of Virginia's former PhD students, Kenda Stewart, now works full time for a Veterans Affairs hospital, doing qualitative work. Another of her former PhD students, Andria Timmer, helped establish a nongovernmental organization while she was still in graduate school. One of Brigittine's former undergraduate students at Grinnell, Claire Branigan, worked in housing rights for immigrants in Minneapolis before turning to graduate school and focusing on femicide in Argentina and the United States. Some of the smartest and wisest anthropologists we have trained and worked with prefer to think of anthropology as a field with great potential to set policy or influence people outside academia.

Interestingly, anthropologists have insisted on such public relevance since the field emerged as a named and identifiable area of knowledge in the late nineteenth century. Certainly, we now cringe at some of the early work done by anthropologists. Franz Boas's collection of sacred objects from Native communities on the Northwest Coast and exhibition of them in urban centers not concerned with or catering to contemporary members of those communities we now understand to be deeply problematic.[3] Likewise with Frederic Putnam's participation in late nineteenth-century world's fairs that exhibited

[2] Miguel Vale de Almeida (born in 1960) is a Portuguese anthropologist, LGBTQ activist, former member of the Portuguese parliament, and a professor of anthropology at the Instituto Superior de Ciências do Trabalho e da Empresa in Lisbon. He is the current editor in chief of the journal *Etnográfica* and member of CEAS-ISCTE as well as the Portuguese anthropological association. He is well-known as the author of *The Hegemonic Male: Masculinity in a Portuguese Town* (published in English in1996) and *An Earth Colored Sea* (published in English in 2004).

Ashraf Ghani (born in 1949) was elected president of Afghanistan in September 2014. He taught anthropology at Johns Hopkins University for a while and then worked at the World Bank before returning to his native country, Afghanistan, to lead Kabul University there and then run for president. He was a foreign exchange student while in high school, and he initially thought he would study law but later earned a BA in cultural anthropology from the American University of Beirut and an MA and PhD in cultural anthropology from Columbia University.

[3] Franz Boas (1858–1942) is widely considered one of the founders of U.S. anthropology. Though German-born, Boas did research on the Northwest Coast of the United States and in British Columbia and trained many anthropologists in the United States.

non-European people as "objects" of interest,[4] and Lewis Henry Morgan's study of the "classificatory" kinship systems of non-Europeans and non-Euro-Americans and writings about them, which used a social evolutionary scheme that treated western Europeans as the norm, the standard of human civilization, and the societies that were most evolved. Taken together, these founding anthropologists reproduced essentialist, ethnocentric, and racialized notions of difference in their professional capacities.[5] At the same time, all these anthropologists were engaged with the world they lived in during their historical moments, and they tried to understand them analytically and change them for the better. Boas was quite concerned with fighting scientific racism, Putnam with challenging Eurocentrism, and Morgan with debunking polygenesis, the popular theory that there could not possibly be a single origin of humanity because people who looked pretty human in his day still were too different and, in his society's eyes, too inferior to qualify as actually human.

This mission of affecting the public is not what most people outside anthropology think characterizes the field, yet it is long standing and persistent for those on the inside. Take Carolyn Sargent, who, as recent past president of the Society for Medical Anthropology and as a professor and researcher, focuses on improving health-care delivery in the United States. Monica Heller, a professor at the University of Toronto who also serves on various cultural and language boards in Canada, rose to the presidency of the AAA, which, as a U.S. association, is rarely headed by anyone outside the U.S. She is dedicated to featuring language issues within the field of anthropology but also outside it. And Tom Boellstorff, who teaches at the University of California at Irvine, writes books based on his research and, as mentioned earlier, was for several years editor in chief of the *American Anthropologist*, also thinks of himself as an activist for LGBTQ people.[6]

The list goes on. Sarah Francesca Green has led European Union teams focusing their research on migration and space and, since moving to Helsinki,

[4] Frederic Putnam (1839–1914) was an important late nineteenth- and early twentieth-century anthropologist at Harvard University. He was quite involved in the world's fairs of his time, such as the 1893 Columbian Exposition in Chicago. Over his long career, Putnam held zoological curatorships, worked with eminent naturalist Louis Agassiz, and directed pioneer field expeditions in Ohio, New Jersey, the U.S. Southwest, Mexico, and Central and South America.

[5] Lewis Henry Morgan (1818–1881) is widely thought to be a founder of U.S. anthropology, along with Boas. Over the years, he has been less influential in U.S. anthropology than Boas, but in his day he was quite influential. Part of a large group of people on both sides of the Atlantic Ocean who were social or cultural evolutionists, he was a lawyer by training and a liberal in the politics of his day.

[6] LGBTQ is the current and preferred acronym to refer to lesbian, gay, bisexual, transgender, and queer people, their nonheteronormative lives, and their social identities.

has also become coeditor of *Social Anthropology*, the journal of the European Association of Social Anthropologists; president of the European Association of Social Anthropologists itself; and head of the AAA's Society for the Anthropology of Europe. And Leslie C. Aiello, who just recently stepped down from the presidency of the Wenner-Gren Foundation for Anthropological Research after a long and successful academic career in London, is now president of the American Association of Physical Anthropology, a position that she hopes will help her influence the way anthropologists relate to the wider public. These are not honorary positions. People who run for these positions or take on major editorial positions work long and hard to improve the quality and the impact of the work anthropologists do, often with little or no remuneration. Editorial positions require reading many manuscripts, sending several out for review by experts in relevant areas of knowledge, and deciding which ones get published. Publishing good manuscripts takes many hours of reading and thinking, but people do it because they want those manuscripts to have an impact.

We say these things to provide an analytic frame, but we also want you to hear how our fellow anthropologists describe these choices themselves. We could do this with each of the many interviewees we feature in this book, but we have chosen a few to include here because we want to stress the singularity of their commitment and their range of choices. In the following pages are perspectives offered by Carolyn Sargent, Monica Heller, T. J. Ferguson, Tom Boellstorff, and Leslie Aiello in their interviews with Virginia.

Here Carolyn provides some context about her work to improve health-care delivery:

> My academic engagement with health and medical systems really took shape in the Peace Corps, when (although I was officially part of an animal traction project to train draft animals) I spent a lot of time at the provincial maternity clinic, hanging out with the government midwives. Their clients were primarily elite women, wives of government officials or wealthy traders. I had what I thought was a bright idea of doing neighborhood outreach, weighing babies around town. The midwives were totally opposed. This and two years' worth of observations at the clinics culminated in my graduate school research on reproductive health. Over the years, my interests have expanded to include bioethics (ten years on two hospital ethics committees), immigrant health, and the national health debate in the U.S. I have a deeply personal engagement with the health insurance debate because I have a daughter with chronic health issues who has been an aspiring actor (now in graduate school, still having a hard time with health insurance!).

Virginia asked her,

If you were secretary general of the U.N. or president of the U.S. or surgeon general of the U.S. or head of the World Health Organization, what would you especially want to achieve (or at least work on)? Or . . . might such a position not appeal to you at all?

Here was Carolyn's reply:

I have no desire to be president of the U.S. or secretary general of the U.N. Head of WHO [the World Health Organization], on the other hand. . . . I'd like to have the authority to prioritize integrated health projects, relying on interdisciplinary teams, including local representation, and taking a broad perspective on a particular health issue (e.g., environmental, preventive, curative). I think of this because I recently listened to a report at our medical school (at Washington University) by a physician who has received a multimillion-dollar grant to eradicate microfilarial diseases in West and Central Africa. The plan focuses only on medication, and the team is not interested at all in crumbling dams that lead to mosquito breeding sites, other mosquito-borne diseases that won't respond to this medication, sleeping nets, local understandings of these diseases. . . . This is a huge and ambitious project in terms of financing and countries involved but regrettably narrow in scope.

Virginia pressed Carolyn further:

You have recently stepped down as president of the Society for Medical Anthropology. Have you, in fact, ever thought of quitting the academy and running for public office? If so, which office might actually appeal to you and why?

To which Carolyn replied,

I have zero desire to run for public office. I am sure that I would hate campaigning and would be in a state of constant disappointment at having to compromise a great deal on positions of principle that matter a lot to me. On the other hand, participating on the SMA [Society for Medical Anthropology] Health Task Force that I started as SMA president is an enterprise that I really value. I hope that we can interest medical anthropologists as well as anthropologists from all fields, academic and practicing, to join our initiative. We're currently exploring the feasibility of creating an infrastructure via which anthropologists could provide (collect, if necessary) data to policy makers in response to requests for information; another idea is to compile digests or abstracts of existing research to make these studies more accessible to legislators, among others.

It was clear in this whole exchange that Carolyn wanted to improve health care in the United States (not to mention elsewhere in the world) but thought she could do this better as an anthropologist than as a politician. In her interview with Virginia, she offered descriptions both of her personal experiences and of a path she wants to pursue.

Like Carolyn, Monica Heller also offered some personal context for her interests, which focus on effecting change around language issues:

I grew up in Montreal, and just as I was getting old enough to wander around the city on my own, public space became an ethnolinguistic conflict zone between French speakers and English speakers, and pretty much every utterance became politically charged, so that is clearly part of it. But I also come from a family of immigrants and refugees for whom language and languages were deeply tied to complicated constraints on life chances, so I was quite explicitly socialized to pay attention to such things. Plus we occupy a social position in Canadian society which doesn't neatly fit the available categories of social organization; we kind of violate conventional and highly salient boundaries, especially in Quebec. So that, of course, brings out a lot of interactional boundary work which is a bit difficult to ignore.

Virginia asked Monica,

What is someone like you—someone with your name—doing being a francophone expert or advocate? Heller????"

To which Monica replied,

Oh dear, "expert"? "Advocate"? But I see what you're trying to get at. So, yes, the name business is part of the not fitting dominant modes of ethnolinguistic categorization, which obviously have profound social reality still. People who, as they say, self-identify as "francophones"[7] ... are always asking me for my life story and constructing their own as uninteresting. So the fit is uncomfortable, which is part of what I like about it, although I do regularly blow my stack at the sweetly innocent othering. It's uncomfortable everywhere, of course, and in that sense I would say I am more of a student of categorization, boundary, and stratification processes in which *la francité* is a key element than a francophone whatever. Why the focus on *la francité canadienne*? For the Canada part, I think it is a form of staking a claim to living in, being part of, the society in which, for complicated historical reasons, I was born (despite Canada's famous

[7] This does not occur so much in Europe, given French republicanism and Belgian and Swiss linguistic boundary crossing.

reluctance to let in German Jews), without giving up the critical distance from nationalism (and especially state nationalism) that comes with the territory of living with the ghosts of Nazism. The francophone part: because of its importance in understanding how ethnolinguistic categories are mobilized to construct class relations in Canada and because it has been the central terrain of production of discourses of nationalism in Canada. Also, partly because it is actually easier for me to move in francophone than anglophone circles in many ways. But in many ways my focus really has been on where the boundary is and how to get a handle on it.

Virginia pursued this a bit but then asked Monica,

Did you ever consider a different profession?

Monica replied,

I actually never really expected to be an academic. I have always been interested in doing something concerning the sets of issues I've described here, without necessarily focusing on a particular form that activity might take. Besides being paid so I don't starve to death. When I was in high school, I had thoughts about interpretation and translation, but that was over quickly after I realized that you never get to actually say anything in your own voice, and that a lot of it is women facilitating communication among men, as though we don't do enough of that already. As odd as it might sound, I expected to work for the state in some capacity; might as well be in the belly of the beast, I figure. But also in Canada we—probably naively—still think the state is our friend. I'm attracted to that tension. I do spend a lot of time in my current capacity doing things involving interlocutors from state and paragovernmental agencies, as well as other stakeholders. For example, at the moment I am a member of something called the *Commission de suivi de la situation linguistique*, a body which advises the Office québécois de la langue française (a Quebec government agency responsible for implementing language legislation) on research. I think that kind of thing is fairly typical [of] people in my field, especially those of us who live in places where multilingualism is a political issue. I have colleagues in places like Catalunya, for example, whose lives look a lot like mine.

Sensing that politics mattered to Monica, Virginia then asked her,

If you were secretary general of the U.N., what would you especially want to achieve (or at least work on)?

Monica replied,

Staying sane. The challenge right now I think is that we are working with a global system which is based on the nation-state as the key functional unit at a time when most of what is happening is really beyond the reach of such strategies, both because of the growing importance of sites and spaces at the edge of the limits of state control or outside them altogether (from private enterprise to religious institutions to looser networks) and because so much of what happens requires thinking in relational terms beyond simple state-to-state interaction. The U.N. is based on assumptions that are getting out of date fast.

Virginia then asked what seemed like an obvious question to her:

Why is a Canadian like you so involved in the AAA?

Monica shared,

It goes back to how I ended up in graduate school in the U.S. in the first place, which has to do largely with the fact that training in what I wanted to do (and how I wanted to do it) wasn't available anywhere else. (There is a lot to be said about why that was the case, but there is no room for that here.) So I first came to the AAA as a graduate student, presenting my first paper at a large (and terrifying) conference (I forgot to breathe and my hands went numb). Over the years I have come and gone; to be honest, there have been times when the U.S.-centeredness of the AAA got annoying or just failed to speak to my concerns. And it is sometimes a bit weird to be part insider and part outsider. But the fact remains that I always learn something at the meetings, which is sort of a basic criterion. More than that, the so-called service dimension has taught me things I would never otherwise have learned, and (notably through the Commission on Engagement with Security and Intelligence Agencies) made me question some of my most fundamental beliefs. As for the details, I was originally recruited to run for a section position by a section president I really liked and figured I'd enjoy working with (which I did), and one thing led to another. I've been challenged and stimulated by the work I've been offered, and frankly find the people I have been privileged to work with terribly congenial, even when we really disagree. I'm also involved in bodies in Canada and in Europe, so that gives me an opportunity to profit from boundary crossing, which, as I have said, I really like to do.

T. J. Ferguson's story is different, but he still made the same basic choices most anthropologists make. He followed a different career path from those followed by Carolyn and Monica, who worked mostly on health issues and language issues. T. J. became an anthropological archaeologist, whereas Carolyn became a medical anthropologist and Monica a linguistic anthropologist, but all three chose anthropology nevertheless.

Respecting those differences and those commonalities, Virginia asked T. J.,

When did you establish Anthropological Research LLC, your research company in Tucson, Arizona, and why? Setting up a company always entails a good level of risk and many small businesses fail within the first year. What made you incur the risk in the first place, and would you do it again now knowing what you know that you didn't at the time?

In response, T. J. told Virginia,

I established Anthropological Research, LLC, in 2001. Prior to that, I had a business partnership with Roger Anyon, and we operated a company called Heritage Resources Management Consultants, LLC. I've been working in the private sector since 1995. Until I accepted a half-time position as a professor of practice at the University of Arizona, I worked from a home office, which I find productive and which lowers the overhead of a business.

There really wasn't much risk in starting a business. We've never had to market our services; people have come to us to request our assistance with research projects. I organized Anthropological Research as a limited liability company, which means anyone who sues me can have the assets in my business bank account but they can't take my wife's house. I'm interested in doing full-time research, so I try to operate without employees so I don't have to spend time on personnel management and other administrative tasks. The risks of being in business are reduced by maintaining adequate operating funds and only drawing money out of the company when I need to meet personal expenses or pay taxes.

Virginia then asked,

You strike me as a thoughtful, organized, and practical person. Some people might say that those are the perfect attributes of a practicing anthropologist, while others might think that a practical person would prefer an anthropological career that is 100 percent in the academy (and includes the possibility of tenure). Are these the perfect attributes of a practicing anthropologist?

T. J. responded,

Along with thoughtful, organized, and practical, you need to add hardworking and intellectually innovative to the list of attributes of successful practicing anthropologists. For most of my career I've wanted to do full-time research, and working in the private sector allowed me to do that. In contrast, university professors typically spend only 40 percent of their time doing research, with the rest devoted to teaching and service. In 2007 I accepted a half-time appointment as a professor of practice at the University of Arizona, which is an untenured position designed to bring people who primarily work in the community into the university. I'm now enjoying teaching and sharing my knowledge of how to do archaeology as applied anthropology with the next generation of anthropologists. I'm still adjusting my work schedule in my private business with my responsibilities as a professor but I now enjoy the best of both worlds.

Pursuing this line of questioning, Virginia then asked him if he had ever thought of running for public office, and if so, which office would actually appeal to him and why. To make things clearer, she added,

Do recent political and legislative actions in your home state of Arizona make you consider running now?

T. J. replied to all of this with insight and clarity:

I did run for public office when I lived at the Pueblo of Zuni, and I was elected to serve on the first school board for a new public school district whose boundaries coincided with the reservation. I was recruited to run for this position by the Zunis I worked with. I don't have children, so it was very illuminating to immerse myself in how schools operate, and the challenges of primary and secondary education. Right now I devote all the time I have to my research, and I'm not interested in running for public office. Given the current partisan politics that characterize both Arizona and the United States as a whole, I don't think I'd make a very effective politician. I'm more interested in solving problems than trying to aggrandize political power for one party or another.

In this response, T. J. raised the critical link between education and public, even activist, work. Teaching is one way anthropologists seek to affect the societies they work in, a fact often lost in the dichotomy between academic and engaged anthropology. There are, of course, many ways anthropologists do so, both inside and outside academic institutions, and most anthropologists spend at least part of their lives working in venues outside academia.

Tom Boellstorff, who recounted his fascinating experience as an LGBTQ activist in Moscow in the early 1990s, is keen to blur the distinction between teaching and activism:

It's not like most kids around the world [who] think they're going to be a fireman or a doctor or something [like that]. Anthropologist isn't usually something that's so well known. So it's typically something that comes to people later in life. But I'm one of those people who had a very strange past in life where I had other intellectual interests but then got really involved doing this, this activism with gay Indonesians, and then sort of picked anthropology because it would give me a way to keep going there and working with them in a sense, and the intellectual interests came out of that.... I don't know that many cases of people who are ten years old and they've decided they were going to do that, except possibly archaeologists or something that's a little bit better known. But anyway, I'm definitely one of the ... kinds of folks who came to it later in life in a sense and by a circuitous route.

Virginia asked him one of her standard questions,

Have you ever considered holding public office, starting an NGO, or devoting yourself directly or fully to political advocacy?

She was somewhat surprised by his answer given the range of work Tom has done, but not totally surprised, because it was clear that he chose anthropology once he found it and that it was through anthropology that he thought he could make more of a difference. Here is Tom's reply:

It's a great question, not surprising at all, but it has a dark side. I was in Moscow during the 1991 coup attempt, working underground with gay activists and then using computers the International Gay and Lesbian Human Rights Commission had brought over (and were in my apartment) to help print flyers for the pro-democracy resistance. I was regional coordinator at the Institute for Community Health Outreach in San Francisco and worked with that organization for many years, and have sat on the board of directors for that organization, Mobilization against AIDS, and others. My first two trips to Indonesia, I wasn't even in graduate school yet; I was an HIV/AIDS and gay activist. I've helped many LGBT and HIV/AIDS nonprofits in Indonesia and still serve on the advisory board for two; one of them had their inaugural meeting in my apartment in 1993. I've also been involved in a lot of community activism in Long Beach, California, where I live.

So on the one hand, activism has been central to my life; indeed, it was my path into academia. On the other hand, we can never forget the strains of anti-intellectualism in American society and never want to inadvertently strengthen them. I think that anthropologists who do no clearly identifiable activist work are completely legitimate, and that intellectual work is valuable on its own terms. It is not being ensconced in an ivory tower but being engaged in the human journey. Not everyone has to take the activist route I have taken, nor do I or [does] anyone else need to take it through our whole lives. Of course, I encourage activist work and see no contradiction between activist work and rigorous intellectual work. So the point is that for me it has been very important, and I encourage others to work for social justice and also for greater visibility for anthropology in public discourse, but also that intellectual work is activism, even if its effects are not always immediately apparent.

Lastly, we share personal and intellectual choices that shaped Leslie C. Aiello's career, which Leslie described when Virginia posed the following question:

You have made some impressive career moves in your life—for example, choosing to go the United Kingdom for your doctoral studies in biological anthropology rather than staying in the U.S. to pursue the degree here, then spending some three decades at University College London [UCL] but returning to the U.S. in 2005 to take up the presidency of the Wenner-Gren Foundation. Looking back at these moves, do you think you were taking big risks each time, or did you just see them as logical choices, or perhaps just as moving pragmatically within the world of anthropology?

Leslie replied,

In retrospect, the career moves that I made were risky, but at the time they seemed to be the obvious choice. The real reason I went to London was to start a new life. My marriage had broken up, I had dropped out of graduate school, and I was teaching at Cal State Northridge on a temporary contract. Gail Kennedy, a Northridge colleague and friend, had just returned from London with a PhD in human evolution. She said, "What's keeping you in LA?" and I asked myself the same question. I was ready for a new adventure, and at that time London was the place to go for human evolution. I was tired of stone tools and had become fascinated with the people who had made them. Human evolution was what I wanted to do, and I became the student of Michael Day at St. Thomas's Hospital, University of London.

The first year (1975) was difficult, but good friends like Peter Andrews and Chris Stringer helped me through it. We were all young, excited to be in

London, and just at the beginning of our careers. After the first year I was hired at UCL on a twelve-month contract, which was extended and extended again—although I had no intention of staying past the completion of my doctorate. But life intervened, the PhD took longer than expected, I met a man (whom I am still with), I was given a permanent contract, and I realized that London was an ideal place for an academic career. I was curious about academic life in the U.S., however, and took a visiting position at Yale in 1986/87. It was a great year, I wrote a major book, and made some close friends, but I also realized that all was not always greener on the other side of the Atlantic, and happily returned to "real life" in London at the end of the year.

Thirty years is a long time to be in one place, and after working myself up through the academic ranks, I began to wonder what more I could accomplish at UCL. These niggling doubts coincided with a downturn in the UK funding environment for human evolution, my husband's decision to take early retirement, and the fortuitous arrival of the Wenner-Gren job advertisement in my inbox. We decided we had another adventure left in us and New York and Wenner-Gren were it. It was quite a jolt moving from an academic environment, however. Wenner-Gren is the first nonuniversity job I have had since I was seventeen and a sales girl at JC Penney's.

Professional Trajectories, Professional Choices

Earlier in this book we drew attention to anthropologists' first encounters with the discipline. Here we have focused on what anthropologists say about choosing anthropology as a profession and committing themselves to it over a number of years. We draw this distinction because encountering something and adopting it or committing to it are very different moments and commitments. For example, Virginia had encountered algebra, geometry, astronomy, history, zoology, and philosophy in high school, but she did not choose to become a mathematician, an astronomer, a historian, a zoologist, or a philosopher in her adult years. Monica Heller and Tom Boellstorff both encountered linguists and linguistics earlier in their careers but chose not to become linguists because anthropology provided a better lens for considering language and its social and political uses. Neither Carolyn Sargent nor Edward Liebow chose to become a physician, although they both were in conversation with the medical sciences during their studies and careers; they found anthropological ways to engage with these fields to be more fruitful, more satisfying, and even more meaningful.

It is both the social aspect of anthropology's questions and the field's ways of answering them that drew these colleagues to it, though many recognize the value of work in other fields and professions. Mary L. Gray provides another great example, since she chose anthropology when people back home in rural

California had what she now calls "practical, vocational degrees—nursing, cooking, hairstyling." Notice how Mary talks about her choice of anthropology once she "found" it and the path it opened into a professional life as she candidly discusses her choice of graduate school and entering into community-organizing work:

I found and fell in love with anthropology and Native American studies the end of my freshman year [in college]—the thick of the political fight over the Repatriation Act.[8] I am sure that I would not have made it through college if I had not found these departments that silently seethed at the existence of the other. Far from abstract or divorced from the world, each gave me equipment for living and ways of seeing power as something that could be moved through people's collective actions.

... I moved to San Francisco to take up a master's degree in anthropology even less certain of what one "does" with an advanced degree in anthropology, but college had proved useful so far. If I'm honest with myself, I know that that degree was a way to get a student loan to live in a city that seemed like a better destination than back to my home town. And I was right. But I also found that I had more than a crush on anthropology—I was deeply in love with the discipline. I took seminars in the evenings and during the day worked at a small start-up called PlanetOut—a media site for LGBTQ people—as its "community architect." I was using my anthropological theory to build queer worlds online. I loved it. And that's when I realized that I could make anthropology my vocation. I would keep studying it so that I could ask the next set of questions that interested me: What difference did the internet make to young people navigating queer identities in places, like my home town, that did not have the material infrastructure, ubiquitous in cities, to plug into an offline gayborhood?

I had spent close to two years doing fieldwork in Southeast Appalachia—a good amount of time in the two states that border Indiana to the east. Until that last year, I did not imagine that I would apply for a tenure-track job. I was focused on my research. I thought I would apply that work to community-based organizations supporting LGBTQ social movements in rural and poor communities, helping them think through how to collectively organize when one does not have the material wealth to control legislative agenda setting. It

[8] The Native American Graves Protection and Repatriation Act is a federal law in the United States passed in 1990 as a result of decades of Native American/American Indian activism for autonomy and self-determination. The legislation mandates that all Native American/American Indian skeletal remains and sacred cultural artifacts held by public institutions be inventoried, that this information be provided to federally recognized tribes, and that the items be returned to them once they have been claimed.

never occurred to me that a quirky department at Indiana University—Communication and Culture—cofounded by a set of scholars at the margins of anthropology studying media technologies might see my research as a fit for their department. Lucky for me, they did. I joined Indiana University as an assistant professor in 2004 and received tenure here in 2010.

But this was not the only move Mary made. For the past several years, she has been working for and with Microsoft, on loan from Indiana University, but imagining the future and labor in a digital world. She retains, however, a strong sense of anthropology as her chosen profession despite this shift from the public to the private sector.

Our main point here is that people choose to become anthropologists, and this typically feels like a lifelong commitment. What people do with it varies, of course, but it is that spaciousness that makes sense to people who choose the field. Some people become anthropologists because of anthropology's openness to questions of many different sorts, questions that made more sense to them than those asked or answered in other disciplines. This intellectual spaciousness often opens up a path that people can merge with their own interests and passions in order to build a career in anthropology over the course of several years. It is also that spaciousness that invites collaboration with colleagues in other fields, which allows anthropologists to discover what those fields can bring to a project. But collaboration also highlights what anthropologists like them bring to each project and each situation that provides a novel and valuable orientation.

It is not that anthropologists are uncritical of some anthropology or of many of the institutions they work for. Many are necessarily so because of the ways in which institutions wield power, but many still love anthropology as a profession, what they believe it can do, what they want it to be and do, and how it differs from other professions. Some of that commitment—even love of the field—comes across as great enthusiasm, bordering on what may seem to be excessive idealism or utopianism because of a shared desire to change the world for the better. But anthropologists are typically realistic about power differentials and patterns of discrimination, so the hope is that anthropology can be a way to live one's life while exposing important issues and fighting for more egalitarian relations, a way of doing something in the world that is both interesting and in agreement with one's values.

We did not anticipate this trend when interviewing such a wide range of anthropologists. But committing to anthropology as a profession may be something people do despite having found it after high school and not earlier in their lives; despite having to deal with the frequent skepticism of family, friends, or classmates who wonder about its viability as a way to earn a living; and despite issues with the field and the institutions in which it is practiced. People often explore anthropology for a while before they really commit to it, but once they do, it becomes a commitment for life, no matter what actual job someone has. In some ways, it is just as much a calling or a vocation as that of a physician or priest. Most of us become anthropologists for life, whatever employer we have and whatever income we manage to get. Once one thinks like an anthropologist, asks questions like an anthropologist, answers them like an anthropologist, and engages with the world like an anthropologist, one becomes an anthropologist throughout one's lifetime.

Virginia has at times been surprised that people in other professions tell her she thinks and acts like an anthropologist. She bristles a bit when they say that because she is not always sure that it is a compliment. But it may be true, and we should think of it as a compliment. It is the training and the commitment to a contextual approach to humanity that deserve praise and the relentless questioning of facile truths that render us recognizable as a distinct profession.

4

Anthropologists' Work, Locations, Institutions, and Successes

•••••••••••••••••••••

As we have already said, anthropologists have many different kinds of jobs, both inside and outside academia, and they generally like their jobs in both cases. In this chapter, we talk about what anthropologists do when they are working in a variety of contexts and focus on how they described this work when we interviewed them. As in all professions, there are good days, bad days, great days, and so-so days in anthropological work. Sometimes it depends on a person's responsibilities, and sometimes it depends on changes in the public sector and their impact on the anthropologist, which is to say that anthropological lives are shaped by the broader sociopolitical contexts in which we function as professionals.

For example, many anthropologists are responsible for, but do not necessarily enjoy, administrative work, so when they chair a department or have to deal with a great deal of bureaucracy, they often complain. This is not true of all anthropologists, as we shall show in this chapter with Edward Liebow's discussion of his own administrative work and why he likes it. Ed went from working with many others at Battelle in Seattle and serving as volunteer treasurer of the American Anthropological Association (AAA) to working in his current position as executive director of the AAA and managing a staff of about twenty people and an organization that exceeds ten thousand members. Clearly Ed has many years of experience managing staff, creating initiatives within large organizations, and keeping an eye on finances from his administrative roles;

these skills were highly desirable and led to his being chosen from among many competitors to lead a major professional organization. This is not unusual in the work many people do in other professions, work that involves management of teams and resources, and it is something often done by anthropologists, too, when they run organizations, head departments, work for government agencies, and run their own businesses. But it is not what most anthropologists particularly enjoy in their work, even if they find it necessary and valuable. It is an aspect of our work that goes unnoticed by people both inside and outside the field, but it is nonetheless central to the practice of anthropology as a profession.

The collective experiences represented in this book indicate unequivocally that most anthropologists love doing research, talking about it, preparing for it, presenting it, and sometimes getting their findings published, albeit in different ways. Many anthropologists also love to teach young people and interested students of all ages in a variety of contexts that may or may not include a classroom. As anthropologists and people who have also run departments and been involved with collegiate administration at various levels, we are both accustomed to evidence of these positive attitudes and results. But we are also aware of frustrations that many anthropologists experience in their work. After all, not all manuscripts get accepted for publication, not all op-eds get picked up by the media, not all students are diligent about their assignments, and not all university or organizational policies help anthropologists do their research, teach, or do related work. So, as we said, there are good days, bad days, great days, and so-so days in anthropology, as in any profession.

Let us give you some examples of the range of work anthropologists do based on our own experiences first. Virginia can certainly think of successes. She remembers them well—establishing the Eileen Basker Memorial Prize in 1987 (and seeing it thrive each year since then), nominating colleagues for major prizes and seeing them win (three such wins in 2017 alone), getting major grants and fellowships (from the Rockefeller Foundation, the Fulbright Program, and the Ford Foundation, for example), seeing colleagues get major grants and fellowships (from the National Science Foundation, the National Institutes of Health, the Wenner-Gren Foundation for Anthropological Research, and even the Gates Foundation, for example), getting a book accepted for publication (such as this one), getting a book nominated for a major book prize, hiring colleagues she has really wanted to hire, retaining colleagues when other institutions have tried hard to get them, connecting really well with students in a course, and getting excellent anonymous course evaluations from students.

But Virginia also remembers failures—getting rejections from national granting agencies and private foundations, getting rejections from journal editors for manuscripts she has written or co-written, being unable to hire a highly valued colleague, being unable to retain a highly valued colleague, not connecting especially well with students in a course, being unable to change a university or organizational policy, and not getting a job she wanted.

Brigittine has similar experiences of successes as well as failures, although those that pertain to teaching and administration are substantially different because of distinct student populations and institutional structures at private liberal arts colleges in the United States. As she discusses later, teaching has been a constant pleasure in her life, while managing conflicts that arise occasionally between students and faculty members in an administrative capacity has been challenging at times.

Both Virginia and Brigittine have been involved in very rewarding and, at times, frustrating institutional governance well beyond the kind of work that one may expect in anthropology departments. Virginia coimagined, codesigned, and cofounded the International Forum for U.S. Studies, which has resided in two different academic institutions, and Brigittine led efforts to create a new area in the curriculum of the Peace and Conflict Studies Program at her home institution. In each case, these efforts took years of planning, deliberating, discussing, and seeking support among our peers and administrators. Likewise, we both have dedicated immense amounts of time to personnel issues: Virginia was part of a high-level search for a university president, and Brigittine served on the institutional committee that reviewed all contract renewals, tenure, and promotion cases. Recruiting, supporting, and assessing the careers of other professionals in and across institutional locations is often an integral part of the work that anthropologists do.

As we write about these professional experiences to render them visible to people interested in the profession of anthropology, we share our conviction of the importance of this kind of work. Yet we both probably need to remind ourselves of all the labor each one of those took—successes and failures alike. These things all take long-term and ongoing work. Each published article has to be based on original thinking, original findings from research, and many hours of writing, rewriting, and editing. Each published book represents between five and ten years of sustained work. Each case of hiring and retention takes hours of face-to-face meetings, interviews, correspondence, and written reports. Our work lives always include a good deal of what Virginia calls "social work"—receptions, dinners, small talk, and diplomatic conversations that are tacitly obligatory parts of our profession. Each grant proposal we submit for possible funding takes preliminary research to make it viable; many hours of reading publications that may pertain to our proposed research; calculation of likely costs; and many hours of writing, drafting, editing, and rewriting before an actual submission to the granting agency, which may or may not look upon the work with favor.

While people outside the academy may tend to think that professors "just teach class," we want to underscore how much preparatory work competent, responsible, and committed teaching takes outside the classroom. We have to conceptualize the whole course before we start teaching it. Most of our courses are our own creations at all levels. We order books and select articles that are appropriate; this means reading and choosing from among many potential books and articles and improvising when they do not work as we imagine. We see students during our office hours and outside them to talk about assignments and ideas, and we extrapolate on students' interests. We assess assignments. We prepare lectures, and we contemplate how well we succeeded in past lectures and what changes we might need to make based on this information. We work to structure discussions in meaningful and balanced ways for our students. All these skills are honed over time and tested in a constant way inside and outside the classroom with our students.

There are common misunderstandings, too, that rarely reflect what anthropologists do at work. Virginia remembers a former graduate student who surprised her and a couple of other students one day by proclaiming that she had never been rejected for anything. It was a surprising moment because that is not the experience the vast majority of us have. We all get rejections. Funding is extremely competitive, even for senior scholars. Often between one hundred and two hundred people apply for jobs we might want. We might put a great deal of time and effort into teaching and not have students see it or value it.

Each institution has rules and regulations that affect anthropologists who work there, and each country has rules, regulations, possibilities, and constraints as well. When Mary L. Gray, now at Microsoft but also at Indiana University, reflects on her work, she notes that the freedom to focus on whatever research she wants is offset by other constraints most of us share. She still has to get a publishing house to agree to publish her work, she has to manage the work of others, and she has to do paperwork needed by Microsoft (and at times Indiana University). That is one of the reasons we have chosen to feature anthropologists from several countries and not just the United States. Monica Heller is in Canada, Sarah Francesca Green is in Finland, Nandini Sundar is in India, Mariano Perelman is in Argentina, and Marilyn Strathern is in England. Each one deals with distinct bureaucratic regulations and cultures. Some of their issues are financial, some are legal, some are organizational, and some are political. These factors also influence our work relative to how governments use, invoke, or reflect public attitudes about social justice, ancient history, human reproduction, higher education, and anthropology in particular. For example, the exchange rate at the moment in Canada and Argentina is not favorable to our colleagues in those countries, so their ability to participate in international conferences is increasingly limited. Many of those who did not vote for Brexit in England are having to deal with the consequences of that referendum for their research, their students, and their connections to people in the European Union. The current move to the Right in many countries has seriously worried many anthropologists around the world—both out of their concern for social justice, inequality, and the protection of minorities and for the consequences these moves can have for the practice of anthropology. Of the anthropologists on whom we draw for this book, this is a major concern for Sarah (at the University of Helsinki), Mariano (an Argentinean anthropologist concerned with labor), and Nandini (at Delhi University).[1]

It is important to think about the time periods anthropologists work in (moments and periods in history), and not just about countries. For years, Virginia has repeated what she heard from Brazilian colleagues under Presidents Luiz Inácio Lula da Silva and Dilma Rousseff—namely, that Brazil was opening up new universities and needed anthropologists. Now, since the latest coup in Brazil, anthropologists and their national association (the Brazilian Anthropology Association) experience threats and attacks much more than expansion and support. Portugal, now under a socialist government, not the long-lasting right-wing dictatorship that many people associate with Portugal, is currently seen by colleagues there as a welcome refuge for people who—like most anthropologists—are arguing against and battling right-wing moves in their own countries, including Poland, India, Israel, and the United States. It is then no surprise that Portugal is one country with a recent history of having an anthropologist serve in its parliament—Miguel Vale de Almeida, having gotten involved in politics over LGBTQ issues, served as member of Parliament in recent years.[2]

In the United States, we have never had an anthropologist in Congress, but some have served as college and university presidents, some have become the heads of museums, some have founded organizations (from Partners in Health to Antropólogos sem Fronteiras/Anthropologists without Borders), and one is the most recent head of the World Bank, Jim Yong Kim, who is both a medical doctor and an anthropologist. Of course, President Barack Obama's mother had a PhD in anthropology from the University of Hawaii at Manoa, and we assume that she had some influence on him. The vast utility of an anthropological perspective in professional life is one major strength of the discipline. We believe in that strength even when the public at large knows little about anthropology.

[1] The September 2017 issue of *American Anthropologist* includes a special section—all written by anthropologists—on this move to the political right around the world. Among the authors are Sarah, mostly writing about Greece, where she grew up; and Mariano, mostly writing about how race and racism now underwrite Argentina's current policies, especially about immigrants and immigration.

[2] There is a wonderful and lengthy interview with Almeida in the March 2018 issue of *American Anthropologist* (Feldman-Bianco and Almeida 2018). It is actually a mutual interview done over email in Portuguese between him and Brazilian Bela Feldman-Bianco (and later translated into English by Virginia).

Now we will turn to hear from some of our colleagues about their jobs, their locations, their institutions, their challenges, and their successes. We highlight and include lengthier excerpts from our interviews because of the range of information and depth of feeling these anthropologists imparted to us. What follow are excerpts from our conversations with anthropologists who work in agriculture in the United States, psychological and medical issues in Brazil, anthropology in Argentina, management of public health research mostly in the United States, a major museum in the United States, and human-macaque relations in different parts of the world as well as administration of funding and mentoring at a major university in the United States.

Jacqueline Comito told Brigittine,

At the end of my master's, I took a year off and I basically worked as a consultant and it was doing a project trying to help understand fire and EMS [Emergency Medical Services]. It wasn't a topic I understood, but I had to. You know I always consider anthropologists like lawyers. We've got to learn something very quickly. If you know the basic good anthropological approach to doing data collection and seeing the world, well, in fact, it's not even about data collection, right? It's about seeing the world. And I think once you go down the path of truly immersing yourself in anthropological literature and in anthropology education, it isn't about our methods. It's about teaching us to change our mind-set about how the world works, and how we can connect the pieces of the world together in a way that makes sense.

What was neat was after I got my master's [degree], I got to start teaching anthropology in community colleges. I did that also that year. And that was a blast. I loved teaching anthropology because I love trying to help other people change their way of viewing the world.

... I didn't mention what my dissertation, or what my master's [research, was] about. I did a life history work on my mom's family. What was really cool about it was that I was able to connect them to a brother who had moved away years ago and they never heard much from him. So after his dad died, they basically, most of them hadn't seen him. So I went out there and met Uncle Dick and interviewed him, and I pulled together all these different stories of each sibling and again sort of what I did in that novel (novella) that I wrote. I did this in real life based on their stories and I created this life history. So it was growing up Italian in a certain period in Des Moines from their perspective.

Brigittine asked,

This time with an anthropological moniker?

To which Jacqueline responded,

Yeah, and using taped interviews, and so again it's showing that obviously in a large family you're always obsessed with this different perspective thing, anyway.

So in 2005 I get approached by a sociology professor at Iowa State to do a short-term baseline study for this conservation-based program that they're doing called Iowa Learning Farm.

Brigittine asked,

Is that because you're a known consultant?

Jacqueline explained,

It was twofold: known consultant and I had also started doing some environmental work. So I was asked. I did this thing called Caring for Creation for Ecumenical Ministries where we actually did some policy work and I brought together all of these people, so I had done that and then they asked [me] to be a guest speaker to go out to the East Coast and do a youth thing on the environment, so I started to get this environmental niche, which was really fascinating, right? And again I had no background [in] EMS and fire, which is what I've been doing. And I grew up in this state but, really, I call it the company store. I had worked for the company store, which is agriculture, right? I did care about the environment, but I wouldn't say it was something I was talking about. I remember when I went to Italy one time and they looked at me and they said, "You guys have bad water over in the U.S., don't you?" and I was like, "I don't know what you're talking about. No? It's fine." And now I work on water quality and I am, yes, we have bad water in Iowa, you know, very bad water in Iowa. So I took this job that was only meant to be part time. It was full time but only six months, so I didn't get any benefits and I had been teaching at Iowa State, so it was one year of doing adjunct teaching of linguistic anthropology. One year [as an] adjunct, and I moved into this new contract. Steve Padgett was the sociologist, a fabulous guy, [and] in six months he taught me so much, again a crash course on agriculture and conservation, and—you know me—I asked a million questions because I was just intrigued.

I was helping educate the people around me about what an anthropologist was and did—what I did different from what Steve did as a sociologist, like we still had to do surveys, because everybody wants to survey. It's what people were willing to pay for unfortunately, quantitative is what [they wanted], because it's tangible more than qualitative. But if you're a good anthropologist you teach them the quality of qualitative research, right? That is part of our job.

In these applied contexts that Jacqueline encountered, she identified the need for social scientific research that is driven by pragmatic and policy concerns and she applied an anthropological toolkit to them with great success.

Now consider the jobs and work of a wonderful academic anthropologist, João Biehl. In his discussion with Virginia, they drew attention to key anthropological skills that translate to a variety of professional activities.

Virginia asked,

Do you think that listening is more important or harder than watching? I have sometimes thought about this, and I realized that maybe, from my own experience doing fieldwork, it is one of the things I heard a lot from my mentor long ago. You were saying that Catarina [an interlocutor with whom João had worked for years] asked you to come over, and you say that there is a force there, but, in some ways, how did you know this?

João responded,

I think there is something very sharp about what you are saying and about listening and observing. And you are absolutely right.... As I have said in the book [*Vita*],[3] there is the language of Catarina and it is a language of uniqueness. But at the same time her language had this literality and all these literal references to people and events and to the world of existence. I found that it is so riveting, you know. In some ways, [it was just riveting] to be drawn to a not-so-clear-cut logical sense of language and the liberation of registers—the real, the imaginary, the symbolic. I think that, even where she was this abandoned creature, she was able to navigate with more creativity the domains and, from that position, she was able to see and perceive the social world. She was able to see what I call the crossroads of life, in which life chances are determined. So the ethnographic work ended up being trying to locate those crossroads....

... I want to tell you that I want to understand what her life had become and see what happened to her and what made her [what she was]. In some ways listening comes in again [and again] and I need to listen to the various parties involved. It was not so easy to find her ex-family and then listen to them. Another layer of complexity came in as I moved into the medical and the domestic worlds in which she has been excluded. And I had to listen to those people, and it was also a difficult enterprise to listen to her family and try to find ways to explain why they had abandoned her in the first place. I had to try juxtaposing all these accounts when I was trying to identify the crossroads in which decisions are made about her sanity or insanity, and whether she was productive and desirable or not. And I like to think of ethnography that is a

[3] João wrote a wonderful, award-winning book largely about social abandonment in Brazil. See Biehl (2005). Much of it follows the trajectory and eventual institutionalization of a woman called Catarina.

people-centered form of evidence as creating a text in which, like, real people jump off the page and then the reader can have a relationship to people, get closer to people. And they are not necessarily hostage of my interpretation or my rendering, or what I might take as a possible decision. So if it's open-ended work, it allows the reader to work. This is not to say that I don't have my own strong opinions about what should be done normatively in terms of policy or morally. But I think what is so powerful is that anthropologists bring people closer to people and not just to the rationalities or to the workings of the world as we see it. . . . Observing the aspects that go along with the listening [is important]. Over the years, in some ways I had the [good] fortune to work with Torben, an artist.[4] It is not always easy but it was a wonderful experience to trust this other person. I think the visual component of things is very important, and I think it does some of the work of observation as well.

Virginia asked,

I am interested in photography, but I also worry about it in fascinating ways. I do not mean that the photographs in your work . . . are not stunning, but I can also imagine people wondering what the function of those photographs really is.

João responded,

You know, Virginia, it is interesting that you raise this in some ways about a lot of my work—maybe it's not just me, maybe a lot more people agree to that—a lot of it just happens, you know. Later you try to make sense and understand. I had to trust that when I saw Torben's work. He got very close [to people] and was able to represent the tragedy in life that is *Vita*. Early on, when we were doing this work, we always thought that this would be a photo book and that I would only write a small introductory essay. It is only when I returned to *Vita* by myself and started to engage more directly [with that work] and in tasks with Catarina that I realized that there was something that only I could do and Torben could not do. I had to unearth, you know, the world [that appeared in] Catarina's words. In some ways, I started to understand better what I could do as an ethnographer and I started to ask less from the photographer.

Virginia then shifted topics with the prompt,

You guys don't use the same name, but Adriana Petryna is your wife.

---

[4] João chose to include many of photographer Torben Eskerod's works in his award-winning book.

João explained,

Yes, she is an anthropologist who works at the University of Pennsylvania, and she has produced wonderful scholarship. Her first book was *Life Exposed* [Petryna 2002], about the Chernobyl nuclear disaster and its aftermath. It basically spawned this powerful concept of biological citizenship. Her next book was called *When Experiments Travel* [Petryna 2009], which is about global clinical research in search of human subjects.

We're working together. The last chapter of her new book happens [to be based on research] in the south of Brazil, where she investigated how people suffering from rare genetic disorders are enlisted in clinical trials and how and whether, when the trial is over, they access treatment, and many times they end up suing the government, since the regional and federal governments cannot continue, or do not want to continue, with compassionate use of drugs. So we are working on a project together on how people are accessing the courts to demand the right to health, which basically means access to treatment, to medicine, and to drugs. This is also one of the outcomes of an intense and positive and wonderful organization, an activist organization for accessing AIDS therapies in Brazil. This was the topic of my book *Will to Live* [Biehl 2007], but that kind of activism has now migrated to other patient groups or diseases, so people from all social backgrounds are going to courts in Brazil to demand their right to health. This is constitutionally mandated [in Brazil], and they are generally successful, at least initially. They get temporary court injunctions, but to settle a case, a lawsuit might take years or decades. So we are building a database in the state of Rio Grande do Sul but also doing ethnographic research.

We are working with sixteen families who are accessing demands [i.e., rights they believe they have]. [They deal with] high-cost genetic therapies and high[-cost] replacement therapies for kids suffering from rare genetic disorders. It is very incredibly moving to hear the medical, social, and now legal trajectories of these families. Most of them are very poor and what they go through in life is incredible, when the kids have a disorder and there might be clinical trials and there might be a therapy. So we are working very closely with these families, and it just crossed my mind that it would be great if [we] could team up with a filmmaker. I actually have a wonderful filmmaker in mind. I adore his work. His name is João Moreira Salles. He is a Brazilian documentary filmmaker. He has made this beautiful, beautiful film called *Santiago*. He is a very good friend of mine. I have not told him about this piece. If he listens to this interview, he will know how much I would like to [work with him].

. . . Something crosses my mind. I think that it is important I know that graduate students are doing this in several graduate programs in the U.S. They are doing visual work. We are trying to do something with our undergraduate students here at Princeton. I am coordinating this program in global health and health policy, and we are encouraging students to do field research early on and then bring this back into the classroom into their junior papers and their senior theses. And actually, next year, we are going to do a full exhibition bringing an African photographer, Damien Schumann, who works on TB [tuberculosis] control in South Africa. He has made portraits and collective life stories, and he has also done films, so we will make an exhibition with Damien, but we will also have our students produce an exhibit of the work that they produced over the summer. So they will be working closely with a curator, Kate Somers, who is wonderful, through the Wilson School here at Princeton. So to make this event, I think it is very important to find alternative ways of expressing what is going on with people in the world. I think the visual media is powerful and an important one. So I'm all there with you, Virginia. I wish I had more time. I wish I were a bit more audacious and I wish I had a camera myself.

Many anthropologists work with and on visual media. João Biehl is not alone. Questions, of course, arise in that context about photographs and films intruding on people's lives but, when people give permission to use photographs of themselves or film footage in which they appear, it is usually because they believe that there is something direct about such images. Some might even say that these images carry a force that words do not convey. Most anthropologists will still see them as representations, not as direct windows onto reality, but images do communicate in ways that seem palpable.

Now consider Edward Liebow's sense of his work at Battelle in Seattle, where he worked for many years before becoming executive director of the AAA in 2013. He highlights perspectives gained and accomplishments earned by working in a nongovernmental organization dedicated to using research to shape policy in the United States:

Well, I was born and raised in the Chicago area. I went to undergraduate school in central Minnesota at Carleton College, and then I moved out to Arizona in 1975 to go to graduate school at Arizona State University, and in 1986 moved here to Seattle to take a position with the Battelle Memorial Institute, which is a not-for-profit research organization and most of its social science expertise is located out here in Seattle, although the institute's headquarters are in Columbus, Ohio. And I have been here [there] at Battelle's Seattle Research Center since 1986.

I think that when you talk to people who have been somewhere for a long time, there are a lot of different factors that contribute to that, but one of the things that [matters is that the] organization is full of remarkably talented people from a number of different backgrounds, so you get a chance to learn something from your colleagues every day. The thing about the applied research world, where our subsistence base largely comes from contracts and grants, is that your work is organized by projects, and so, although you may work for the same organization for a long time, your work life is really parsed into individual projects and at any point in time, I may be working on two or three longer-term research projects. The variety is immense, and the opportunity to do different things and to learn and grow into adjacent intellectual and policy-related spaces expands over time, and so, while I've been at the same place for a long time, I certainly have been doing lots of different things over that time.

Virginia asked him,

Can you think of something that really stands out in the last few years or even since you started working for Battelle that you still relish? The memory of either working with people or somehow really affecting public policy or something else? It could be the people you worked with on a project or it could be that you managed to solve something. Many of us who sit more in academia sometimes are envious of people who might have a closer connection to public policy and the ability to affect it.

Ed responded,

Well, among the things that are quite memorable is the big program that I direct right now [that is, while he worked for Battelle], with sponsorship from the U.S. Centers for Disease Control and Prevention, which has to do with improving the quality of clinical laboratory medicine operations in the United States. It's directly relevant to policy and to health-care improvement. It's entirely consistent with a long-term research focus that I've had, that has to do with how people from different backgrounds come to judge health hazards and risks and effective treatment paths based on evidence that they consider to be credible and acceptable and actionable. . . .

I have been working over the last six years or so with a group of clinical pathologists and laboratorians and learning how they view the world and what they take to be credible evidence for improving the way that they do tests to help inform medical diagnosis and treatment. So this is work that directly contributes to evidence-based recommendations for best practices that laboratorians are asked to follow, and there ultimately may be a payoff in terms of reducing errors, increasing the timeliness and accuracy with which laboratory test results are reported to be able to get patients on the right treatment modalities quicker, and also managing costs by reducing the unnecessary duplication of tests that were done poorly or specimens [that] were misidentified earlier. So in terms of the current context of health reform and quality improvement in health and medicine, this is a very exciting and, I think, important contribution that we have to make.

Virginia then asked,

Is this work right now really one focusing on medical labs, labs in hospitals, or at research facilities, or would you extend it to laboratories in general?

To which Ed responded,

Well, it is—all of the above. There is a law in the United States called the Clinical Laboratory Improvement Act,[5] which governs just about all certified laboratories. It doesn't govern physician office laboratory activities. If you go in and have a sore throat and a provider swabs your throat and does a test right there to see whether that might be a strep infection, for example, that's not governed by this law, but most other testing that's done outside the physician office is under this legislative and regulatory authority. So it includes hospitals, and it includes labs to which tests, specimens, and samples are referred. These are called reference laboratories. And specialty labs as well. Yes, so it's the whole universe of laboratory testing, and of course, in other settings outside of the United States, the same issues prevail, and we depend, in this project having to do with best practices in laboratory medicine, on colleagues in a number of different locales outside of North America, including, Korea, Italy, and Australia. . . .

I do not have any training—any formal training—in public health, and I think it's actually relevant to this discussion and a testament to one of the axioms of anthropological training and application of how I've come to be in this position.

I was first hired [after] I had done a dissertation research project having to do with urban Indian people in the Phoenix, Arizona, metropolitan area and the history of social demography and social network structure. So [I worked on] residential mobility patterns and especially cycling back and forth between the city and the reservation settings from which most Indian people or their families come.

---

[5] Here Ed is referring to the Clinical Laboratory Improvement Amendments of 1988. These instituted regulations that included federal standards applicable to all U.S. facilities or sites that test human specimens for health assessment or to diagnose, prevent, or treat disease. It was an amendment to the Public Health Service Act, in which Congress revised the federal program for certification and oversight of clinical laboratory testing. Two amendments were made after 1988, but the law continues to be cited as the Clinical Laboratory Improvement Amendments of 1988, as named in the legislation.

When I was first hired at Battelle, it was [therefore] directly related to this knowledge base in social demography. I was asked to help recalibrate some models that estimate how much radiation exposure American Indians on the Columbia River plateau might have been exposed to as a result of their living in the vicinity of nuclear weapons fuel production, and a Hanford nuclear site.[6] And everything we knew, even into the mid-1980s, about the health effects of exposure to radiation had basically come from observations of the people who had been exposed to the weapons being detonated in Japan at the end of the Second World War and then some other device testing that had taken place, principally in Polynesia and Australia. And so those were acute exposures, not this sort of chronic, long-term exposure. We knew at the time that the assumptions we were making to estimate exposures were wrong and didn't take into account non-Eurocentric assumptions about lifestyle and behavior patterns. So I was originally hired to help recalibrate these dosimetry models that were used to estimate how much radiation Indian people in the Pacific Northwest might have been exposed to, based on different assumptions about distance from the source, shielding from the source, nutrition patterns, and demographic mobility patterns. That's a fundamental problem in what public health people would call environmental health—that is, the health effects of environmental exposure to harmful chemicals, in this case radioactive chemicals.

I think it's axiomatic among anthropologists that we listen to the people. The people will tell us what's important to them. And in listening to the people, part of my job was training community members in nine tribal groups that were downwind and downstream of the Hanford nuclear works out here in the Pacific Northwest. Among the things that they were concerned about was the impact to environmental resources, but also the impact to their health of exposure to these radioactive chemicals. And it was through years and years and years of trying to get people from the public health and natural resources world in tribal America to work with one another to solve this problem that I came to learn more about public health issues and the public health service apparatus in this country. . . . So it was really just, for me, [a matter of] listening to the people and working with public health officials.

I eventually moved from the environmental organizational unit within Battelle to a public health unit, and, ironically, because I'm not trained in public health, I felt personally that one of the ways that I could help contribute to the organization's success within this public health group was not in doing

[6] Hanford, Washington, was one of three places in the United States where nuclear research was conducted during the twentieth century (along with Oak Ridge, Tennessee, and Los Alamos, New Mexico).

research which I obviously am not trained to do, but to become a research director.

Virginia asked,

Why? What does that mean? I think you said in your written answers that you now manage about seventy staff members. You don't just do that, right? You're very good with people. I see this at work, but is it also that in directing such an organization or part of the organization you get to sort of hand-pick which projects you guys prioritize?

Ed explained,

I guess I consider myself the human lab test, or a standard of reasonableness. If people can explain to me [something] in terms that I can understand, what their interests are, or what opportunities they're interested in pursuing, whether the approach that they're proposing is likely to succeed, I think by my being there as an active listener, it helps them do a better job.

Ed reminded us of ways a well-trained anthropologist works with others and can be useful to others. It is not just the topic or area of anthropology that matters. It is also the careful way anthropologists listen, observe, ask questions, and work with many different kinds of people that we want readers to notice here.

And now consider Alaka Wali, who was born in India but became a Latin Americanist responsible for materials and artifacts that were collected in often very problematic circumstances. She stated,

I came here [to the Field Museum in Chicago] as curator of South America and Central America and ethnography. That was my collection, which makes sense, but since I am the only anthropologist on staff, I have been very involved in issues of repatriation. As part of the work I've been doing at the center—the Center for Cultural Understanding and Change that I was the founding director of—we had done a lot of outreach to urban Indian communities and Native American communities here in Chicago. And so I had this connection to Native North America that way. But so, when we were thinking about how [to] reconfigure the territorial responsibilities, I said I would be interested in taking the Native North American ethnography collection. . . . I was interested in thinking about how [to] transform the use of that collection. What does it mean to not just have the object here but to really begin to help and facilitate access to these things originating from North America? I was [also] interested in taking it because I want to expand the concept of the Field Museum to explain what North America has been in that collection. How long are we going to be talking about them as pertaining only to the Native American Indian cultures when North America today obviously is a much broader canvas, and two hundred or three hundred years from now what is it that will interest researchers or publics about North America, right? We need to think about that. Once collections are curated, theoretically they are here for all time. It is very interesting now in the next four or whatever years. I stay here in building a collection of urban artifacts, objects, and their contexts—and not just objects or visual documentations. We can take collections in a very different way now because of the technologies available to us and really rethink things about what it takes to have a collection here, and that is what we are about to start for lack of a better and more imaginative thing. [We label it] the Playful Material Culture Collection.

When Virginia interjected, "It's not a bad name," Alaka replied, "It lacks a little punch." Virginia responded,

It lacks a little punch? I don't know. Maybe, but I still like it. But tell me something. In terms of the word *curator*, it is great to hear what you are talking about. I think many people might suspect a curator mostly takes care of designing and fine-tuning displays—the exhibits the general public sees when they come to a museum. How much of that is the case versus the behind the scenes? Let's say, as much as the preservation of existing objects, but also thinking about collecting new objects, dealing with potential donors [in] trying to raise the money to collect something, and rethinking what kinds of things, if any, a museum should collect. What would you say is the actual general and typical balance of the job of the curator at a major museum? I think it is different at the very small museums.

Alaka explained,

Right. Ironically, when I came here as well, that whole relationship between curatorial authority and display had changed. Curators were less and less the central authority on exhibits and more and more being relegated, if you will, to being what they now call content specialists. But we really don't have much say over how the exhibit will look or, you know, the design and so on of an exhibit. So it has become much more of a struggle, in fact, for curatorial participation in it. In a sense, in general, I think, the curators themselves also took this term away from so much of doing direct work for the collection and the objects for either display, [which] used to be kind of their territorial role. [They used] to publish a catalog of the object without much theory behind the catalog, if you will. So in the 1980s I would say that began to change as well, and curators were increasingly building their reputations on active research, field research, not just based on doing collections research and especially for cultural anthropologists.

It is very difficult to do good, solid research with the collections here because the collections are haphazard. [They are] not very contextualized; they are really dependent on the whim of whoever accepts them or what was given or how it was given, or sometimes we don't have very good extension records, so to think that somehow you're going to say something about a particular group [of people] based on what we have here is pretty ludicrous at this point. That's not the kind of research you can do at the museum. This is a problem for all of us, including for the archaeologists who are here, as well the notion that you need to continue to do solid field research in order to continue to [see] the insides. So the curators' focus [needs to be] their research for more fundamental questions that museum anthropology propels you to think about. The relationship between humans and [their] environment. . . . Those are the questions that basically I think many anthropological curators in large museums are concerned with as kind of their work, if you will. And that is very different from the cataloging of collections or the construction of display, although I do think that representing cultures is an important aspect of public education work that curators do.

Virginia then shifted topics, asking,

Alaka, before you moved to the Field Museum, you had a tenure-track position as a faculty member, right? How would you compare the kind of job you do now with the kind of job you were doing then?

Alaka observed,

There are some big similarities. I mean we're all doing research. We try to publish equally. We do publish our research so there is not a difference in terms of research and publication between a university professor and a curator these days. As a curator, you are judged on your research and publication record as much as any university professor would be. The main difference is in terms of your setting. [Here] you are concerned about a larger public, whereas, as a professor, I was concerned about my students and making sure I trained a few students. Here I've had an impact, or been able to think about an impact that is much broader, not just with visitors who come to the museum but because I am in the position where I have been able to do a lot of work with community organizations in Chicago or Indigenous communities in South America. So I feel like I have been able to do work that is much more varied than the professor would be or has been able to—not to be critical. I guess I can be critical.

Many anthropologists are like Alaka in that they work in museums. They are curators, directors, staff members, researchers, and administrators. Sometimes they combine several of these roles, much as Alaka has over the years. Sometimes they work at smaller museums; sometimes they work at museums called "natural history" museums, as the Field Museum used to be called. Sometimes they work at history museums, archaeology museums, or even art museums. But in all cases they are anthropologists in their research and their engagement with the general public, as well as with colleagues trained in other fields. They do not typically consider themselves academic anthropologists but, as Alaka explained, they see themselves as doing research as well as teaching, just not in a classroom.

Now consider the perspective offered by Mary L. Gray, who also began working in an academic position, achieved tenure, and then chose to take her anthropological career in a different direction:

I got tenure at Indiana University, and my research on the politics of queer visibility and internet use was relatively well regarded. I had established myself as one of the few scholars doing anthropological research about media and technology. I took a leave from IU to join Microsoft Research's New England lab [the MSR Lab], based in Cambridge, Massachusetts, recruited to be part of the Social Media Collective in 2012. Our research group examines the social implications and cultural impact of emerging media (no matter the timing of its arrival). Microsoft Research, while underwritten by Microsoft Corporation, is a center for independent research. Following the tradition of Bell Labs, we maintain complete academic freedom and measure our contributions by our impact on academic and public scholarship.

So what do I do at Microsoft Research? This is perhaps the hardest thing to explain because, in fact, I and my colleagues from computer science, economics, physics, and mathematics also recruited to the MSR Lab do research that we feel needs doing. Some of us work on graphons and think about how phase transitions might help us better model social networks. That's not me. Me? For the past five years, I've collaborated with a computer scientist to study the lives of people training artificial intelligence and how their experiences of distributed, contract-based labor help us better understand the relationship between automation and the future of work. Underlying the question of "What do you do at Microsoft Research?" is a subtle (sometimes not-so-subtle) assumption that whatever I'm doing, surely Microsoft wouldn't fund it if there wasn't something in it for them. Microsoft Research remains doggedly committed to the idea that basic research—the state of the art in computer science—will, eventually, benefit Microsoft. But they are making a deep investment. They have the means and luxury to do that in ways that rival most universities. That has become less true at other tech industry–based labs but, as more social media companies come to accept that they are building social environments, they too seem more interested in allowing social research to progress, untethered from a specific product goal.

Many of us find Mary's apparent total freedom hard to believe. She does note that most universities today are not exactly like that, but the research universities have a history of encouraging basic research. Much of this may be changing as a result of increasingly neoliberal and corporate models for higher education, but most anthropologists firmly believe that anthropologists should be able to do their research and teach based on their interests and values. Many choose to work for organizations whose principles they value, or organizations that understand that anthropologists bring useful skills with them.

Another good example is Douglas Hertzler. Doug began his formal career with a nonstandard academic position that involved a good deal of administration and no tenure possibilities. He then took a position with the international nongovernmental organization ActionAid, as he explains:

One of the neat things about ActionAid [is that] it's one of the few organizations of its size that has a policy, at least at present, of not taking any USAID [United States Agency for International Development] contracts, but that means when you take the position it becomes hard to fund a lot of kinds of international work.

How I came to be where I am now . . . I did a long period of field research back in Bolivia for my dissertation, and I took a long time to write it. Part of it was I just enjoyed the fieldwork experience and enjoyed being in Bolivia and back with some of the same communities I worked with back then but able to focus on really understanding the issue and working with them on the struggles they were having. So that period just took a while, and when it seemed like it came time for me to finish the dissertation and find another job, I actually wasn't quite finished with the dissertation. I got a job with Eastern Mennonite University back in Washington, DC. We were living in Georgia, my wife and I—Jodi Beth—when I was finishing up the dissertation, but she was ready to move on from that. The job she had there . . . The academic job search, when you're under pressure or you don't want to move your family just anywhere . . . This seemed like a great opportunity. But it was a very unconventional position because it involved a lot of administrative duty, running essentially an internship program with an academic component in Washington, DC, and it was year-round, both semesters and the summer and a lot of responsibility for student life issues in addition to teaching. This is all to say that it wasn't the kind of position where I could do much research. But it was a very rewarding position, both in the kind of ways I was able to interact with undergraduates and learning about, you know, the city and the centers of power globally. Helping students find internships with all their interests, I tried to steer a lot of them towards urban social justice issues in community-type placements rather than necessarily, you know, the centers of global power, but plenty of students were interested in—well, in all sorts of things, so I learned a lot about global and local organizations and issues through that whole process. And I'm extremely proud of what some of my students accomplished coming out of that period. Some of them became real key activists in certain areas. It was a good fit. But eventually I was kind of burned out because I didn't get the summers off and there wasn't time to do research yet there was at least some pressure to do some but there wasn't any time to do it.

But I did eventually get to associate professor level there and was thinking about applying for the promotion to professor, but I was just burned out and so I started trying to think. I didn't want to go searching all over the country for a job. Obviously, the ability to move from that job into another academic one would have been a bit limited there in Washington, DC—although I did interview for a position at George Mason University. But one organization I had learned about in the course of placing students was ActionAid, and at one point when a position became open there, I applied for it and I actually didn't get it. I came in second, I guess. I didn't have experience, you know, talking to members of Congress very much. I had a little, actually. I'd had breakfast once with Nancy Pelosi in Bolivia, but that's another story.

But, you know, compared to people who do advocacy work and work with this stuff, I didn't have a lot of experience, so I didn't get the job right away. But the second time a position came open was actually where they really wanted someone to work on land issues. They already had thought about me. So that was about a year later. They called me back and said, "Would you like to interview again?" and so that's when I made the transition. And I was really ready for a change of pace. And it's been very interesting. One thing that's hard about it is [that in] this kind of work the funding is sometimes shaky, so it doesn't have the job security that a tenure-track faculty position has. But it's worked out well for me so far. But it's been very interesting. I get to work with people with global social movements and, for example, I get to talk with activists in Guatemala. Right now, I'm working a lot with Guatemala and Brazil.

ActionAid is global in scope and has offices in about forty-five countries. And it's organized around a federation model, where there's an international secretariat in Johannesburg in South Africa. Its origins are in the UK but, in about 2000, the organization kind of took steps to really try to decolonize itself, if you will. And one of the parts of that was its international secretariat becoming of the Southern Hemisphere, if you will, and the leadership is almost exclusively from the Southern Hemisphere now. The executive director for some time has been a Brazilian, and he works out of Johannesburg.

Doug's perspective highlights a long-term engagement with global economic processes, a perspective that structured part of his administrative work, his teaching, and now his international policy efforts. While his jobs have been diverse, this analytic focus has remained a strength that he has self-consciously cultivated over time.

We want to highlight that this kind of commitment and such mixtures of work experience are not limited to one kind of anthropology. We also see it in applied medical anthropologist Edward Liebow, museum curator Alaka Wali, and communications specialist Mary L. Gray, as well as in biological anthropologist Agustín Fuentes, who works at the University of Notre Dame as a professor but also in governance, leadership, and administration, which all require balancing different jobs and responsibilities. In his interview, Agustín stated,

In a few weeks, I will be in a major conference on peace, war, and aggression in Leiden, in the Netherlands. So yeah, I am traveling. The stars aligned for better or for worse to have me traveling substantially pretty much every month.

Virginia asked,

Are you simultaneously teaching and figuring out how to do that?

Agustín responded,

Yes, I have a near-full-time administrative position. I teach only one class a semester because of the administration. [But] with all of my traveling this entire semester, I am missing a total of three classes. In Kyoto I was there presenting in the biannual international primatological society meetings. These are top meetings for primatologists and they are truly international, so this was full—all primates all the time for five days there in Kyoto. But I was at the EASA meetings [the biennial conference of the European Association of Social Anthropologists] at the invitation of Tim Ingold for a very, very fascinating symposium on human becomings. To be honest, [yes,] it is a social anthropological gathering, but many of the topics are of great interest to me . . . I like to consider myself an anthropologist first and a biological anthropologist or primatologist as part of what I do in anthropology. And so pretty much I like to think that very little is off-limits to me as far as interests go in anthropology.

Virginia pursued this, asking,

So, do you think of yourself in some ways as perhaps a more open-minded and broader [anthropologist] than most anthropologists, including most social and cultural anthropologists? I am smiling because I say this thinking that, OK, you include humans and you think of yourself as someone who is an anthropologist who clearly also thinks about humanity, but you don't limit yourself to humans, unlike most of the rest of us.

Agustín stated,

Exactly. And so I don't think anyone—anyone or everyone else—has to go beyond just thinking about humans or even particular things about humans. I think it is a valid anthropological question to extend the gaze a little bit past our own worlds to the worlds related to organisms like primates. I think the other interface is also one of the most important [and] exciting areas in anthropology. So, in short, yeah, I like to think of myself as open-minded. I think many anthropologists are, but I think [in] our current system, particularly in graduate schools, [people] may be asked to overlimit the range and full potential that anthropologists could be doing to point at something.

Virginia then shifted focus to ask,

What is this more administrative position—institutional position—that you have in Notre Dame right now?

Agustín explained,

I am the director of the Institute for Scholarship in the Liberal Arts. [It's a] fantastic institute. Very unique. It is an institute that resides within the College of Arts and Letters, and Anthropology is in Arts and Letters. We are a dual internal and external funding agency; that is, our charge is to enhance and facilitate the scholarly and creative activity of the college. We do that by providing a substantial [amount of] internal funding support for research, travel, and creative activity for faculty, graduate students, and undergraduates. We also have specialists that work one on one with faculty, enabling [them] to seek access to external funding, grants, fellowships, things like that. Notre Dame is at the very top of NIH [National Institutes of Health] fellowships, and we do quite well in the variety of humanity and social sciences arenas. This is my third year doing this. Yeah. And a few years before that, I was the director for undergraduate fellowships.

Virginia then prompted Agustín with the following:

There's something that you do or have been doing for, I don't know, two or three, four years with undergraduates at AAA meetings.

Agustín responded,

Since even before I was doing my PhD [at Berkeley], I was interested in working with undergraduates. As an undergraduate I had the opportunity to do undergraduate research, so I've been very active in facilitating, mentoring, and fostering undergraduate research. Deborah Rottman, who is here at the Department of Anthropology at Notre Dame, and I have been putting together for over the last five years these undergraduate poster sessions, which I helped organize initially back in 2000 and 2002 when I was still at Central Washington University. There was a very supportive [program there] of having undergraduate students come and give poster sessions. I think it has been an incredible opportunity for undergraduates, but also I think for people to realize the power of undergraduates, their capabilities there as more than just students. And also to push the idea of the poster is not a bad way to present information and engage in a kind of discourse that maybe the podium presentations are unable [to do].

Virginia asked,

I know that your work, your fieldwork, has been in two or three different— very different—parts of the world. Is that based on where macaques live or something else?

Agustín explained,

For about the last twelve years, a lot of my fieldwork has been looking a lot at macaque interactions throughout Southeast Asia, but really humans and macaques have overlapped through Southeast Asia and southern China and throughout the entire Indian subcontinent, or right into eastern Pakistan and Afghanistan. No one mentions that, but they are also there and, of course, in Gibraltar and North Africa. We have this huge array of regions with cultures, religions, and economies, political contexts that are pretty neat comparative tools. So my long-term research projects have been in human-monkey attraction in Mali, Gibraltar, and now also Singapore. . . .

My partner, Devi, is a writer and director, very well known in independent horror comedy and the independent horror genre. And so I've collaborated with her in a number of films and played multiple roles in the film. Not acting but [other things]. I've produced a number of them [films], generating the funds and sort of making sure that things go straight, and I've done a lot of the paperwork and on-set work. I've done sound work and production management work and all of that. I've got a handle on what goes on, but more importantly, I interact with a lot of people in the film worlds, so I have a much better idea what goes into the construction of this visual imagery and these visual pieces, these half-hour pieces, the one-hour films, the short films, the feature films, and that makes it much less scary to me, I think. I have a much better idea [that] there is an enormous amount of manipulation but that manipulation can also be manipulated to our benefit sometimes.

Virginia asked,

Hmmm. Do you have a great example of something we should all go watch that you had a hand in?

Agustín said,

Well, we have a number. Probably the best film that I helped produce—at least that is all I did really—is *Death in Charge*, which is Devi Snively's creation two short films ago, and it has done incredibly well. It has been in nearly one hundred festivals and has won all sorts of prizes, so there is a website for it that I recommend people take a look at. It is a good one and it does invoke a lot of things we talk about in traditional anthropology courses for sure.

Agustín reminds us that anthropologists often care a great deal about many facets of anthropology but that they also care about their own research while simultaneously caring a great deal about other people's research. In this case, we see an anthropologist committed to advancing the work of fellow faculty members but also students, including undergraduates and not just graduate students. We even see that this extends to his partner's work in film.

Lastly, we turn to Mariano Perelman, who underscored the importance of elected service and leadership in voluntary professional organizations, work that is both a great honor and a great responsibility:

I believe that participating in our associations is part of our commitment to research and the anthropological community. Associations are spaces of belonging. They are places in which we can generate spaces for discussion through which to achieve visibility in public venues. It is for that reason that I have decided to participate in national associations (such as the College of Graduates in Anthropology), as well as international associations (such as the AAA and EASA, among others, and at the moment LASA [the Latin American Studies Association]). I think about the need to contribute to the dissemination of Argentinean anthropology in other [national] venues as well as being part of an international scientific community. The commitment to what anthropologists do has made me participate actively in various venues. I have also stopped being a member of some associations because I have disagreed with their organizational structures. On the other hand, sometimes the conditions of our work, life, and place of residence have a lot to do with this commitment [I feel] to belong and participate in [our] associations.

Also, participation in [these professional] associations and the events they organize is key to the production of knowledge. To participate in [professional] associations is a very important [form of] growth and development. This is perhaps one of the key problems we have (speaking for those of us who live in countries where there is no funding for these events or spaces).[7]

Reflections: Analytic Perspectives, Skills, and Trajectories

We have chosen these particular anthropologists because of their range of jobs and what they say about their work and their contexts. We have here someone who works in agriculture but was not specifically trained to do that when she was in undergraduate or graduate school, though she adapted well using anthropological methods and now loves that work. We also have here someone who has chosen to do fieldwork largely in the country in which he grew up, but not on his own family or in familiar settings. He is also married to another anthropologist, who has done anthropological fieldwork both in the former Soviet Union and on pharmaceutical trials around the world, and with whom he now works collaboratively. We have also included here a longtime practicing anthropologist who is now the executive director of the AAA but who spent years leading research teams on important social topics like health issues and nuclear testing, and yet another who practices in the field of critical international development efforts modeled on leadership from the Global South. All of these careers are engaged in different ways with understanding the human condition

[7] Creo que parte de nuestro compromiso con la investigación y la comunidad antropológica es participar de nuestras asociaciones. Las asociaciones son espacios de pertenencia. Son espacios en los que se pueden generar espacio colectivos de discusión en torno al quehacer antropológico pero también se pueden generar espacios de discusión para lograr visibilidad en ámbito público. Así, he decido participar en asociaciones nacionales (el colegio de graduados de Antropología) como internacionales (AAA, EASA, entre otras, en su momento el LASA) pensando en la necesidad de contribuir con la difusión de la antropología argentina en otros espacios así como poder ser parte de una comunidad científica internacional. El compromiso con el quehacer antropológico me ha hecho participar activamente de varios espacios. Al miemos tiempo, he decidido por desacuerdos con formas de organización dejar de ser parte de algunas asociaciones.

Por otro lado, el compromiso de pertencer y participar en asociaciones a veces se ve permeado por las condiciones de nuestro trabajo, vida, lugar de residencia. Por otro lado, la participación en las asociaciones, y en los eventos que organizan son centrales para la producción de conocimiento. Participar de asociaciones es un crecmiento muy importante. Es esto quizás una de las dificultades centrales de los que vivimos en países donde no existe presupuesto para la realización o participación de espacios.

in ways that are concerned with creating stronger, sustainable, and more just communities at different levels.

In addition, we have included someone who started out in the academy teaching and doing research but now works within the museum world to help it decolonize its exhibits and holdings, along with an anthropologist who also began in the academy but then shifted to research in a business context. These two anthropologists' professional lives show the shift from a traditionally expected career to careers that have gone in substantially different directions. We have included someone who does research and some teaching but is also passionate about working with and for professional anthropological associations, both domestic and international, in order to advance the profession in more structural ways. And we have included two colleagues who have a foot in the academy but largely work for nonprofits outside it, showing how it is possible to straddle multiple professional communities successfully. Lastly, we have also included someone largely trained to observe primates outside zoos in natural settings but who thinks of himself as an anthropologist broadly trained in and comfortable with biology.

Listening to Edward Liebow, Douglas Hertzler, and Jacqueline Comito is a wonderful way of understanding the work done by anthropologists who work outside the academy, especially for students envisioning possible careers and the kinds of work entailed in them. Listening to Alaka Wali is a wonderful way to understand what an anthropologist can do when employed by a major museum, and the appeal such a position has personally and professionally. Listening to Mariano Perelman is a wonderful way to see how an anthropologist might think about research and writing but also about being active in professional anthropological associations. Listening to Mary L. Gray is a terrific way of seeing how and why an anthropologist might work well in an interdisciplinary research unit sponsored by an organization in the IT world. And listening to João Biehl and Agustín Fuentes is a wonderful way to see how listening, watching, and revisiting sites helps anthropologists of all sorts come to conclusions about human life, human actions, and the importance of teaching these to others. We know that every day is not necessarily a rosy day for any one of these people, any more than it is for people in many professions, but it is quite interesting to see and hear the enthusiasm many of these anthropologists have for the skills and approaches they learned and have applied as anthropologists over the course of many years. Some may have gone into anthropology because they saw it as a way of doing research—social, linguistic, applied, medical, archaeological, or biological. Some went into this profession because they saw themselves teaching in the classroom, through exhibits, or by working directly with others outside anthropology. Few went into anthropology to do administration, to be honest, but many have found it necessary in order to advance their own work or the work of others from a more institutional vantage point.

Interestingly, too, many have zigzagged a bit, or even a lot, in the jobs they have had or the responsibilities they have taken on, but none of these people has found that zigzagging to be a way out of anthropology. On the contrary, they find that the multiple roles they play, and the mix of responsibilities they have, demand skills and approaches they learned while training to be anthropologists and in jobs they have had as anthropologists. In other words, such professionally diverse lives show both the depth and breadth of anthropological lives.

5

Anthropologists' Passions, Frustrations, and Challenges

• •

Most anthropologists we know casually, professionally, or personally are passionate people in some way. As we will see in the reflections offered in this chapter, those passions are diverse and eclectic, yet all of the anthropologists involved in this project expressed deep passions for their work, which does not necessarily mean for their jobs. Rather, their passions for anthropological work have to do with social commitments, individual experiences, challenges to inequality, and the questions anthropologists feel compelled to answer in their own unique, yet disciplinary, ways.

Anthropologists also have passions that, though they are not related to their work in obvious or even intuitive ways, point to rich lives beyond the professional, and these passions are worth considering. We have noticed, though, the ways in which the anthropologists featured in this book make connections between their passions and their anthropological lives in unexpected and interesting ways. Of course, several of our colleagues also articulated a great passion for anthropology itself, something related to the common secular vocational drive to become an anthropologist that many colleagues hold, which we highlighted in chapter 2. Tom Boellstorff's perspective resonates for many of us in the field who are living professional anthropological lives: "I love anthropology. I love doing the research. I love writing. I love doing it. To me it's a constant joy and I just, you know, feel so fortunate that I get to do this kind of work."

We appreciate that passion and the privilege to pursue it are dually linked in this frequently shared perspective.

A striking commonality among the anthropologists' perspectives represented here is a concern for anthropologists' public engagement and dissemination of anthropological knowledge to different communities well beyond the academy. For some of our colleagues, these related themes were sources of great satisfaction and joy; for others, they were major frustrations and enduring challenges that they faced as they reflected on their careers. We explore both perceptions of anthropological public engagement; this topic will serve as the bridge between the initial discussion of anthropologists' passions in the beginning of this chapter and the subsequent discussion of anthropologists' frustrations and challenges in the second part of it. In other words, public engagement occupies two sides of the same coin in many anthropological lives.

Despite the deep passions anthropologists are quick to articulate, there are a good deal of frustrations and challenges they experience both within and outside the discipline. Those center on broader social questions about inequality, injustice, and lack of transparency or truth in some facet of human life. In fact, the pursuit of anthropology as a professional path may well be linked to notions of the discipline's particular analytic tools for raising questions about the social world that we often find quite troubling and sometimes underscrutinized from lived perspectives. Linguistic and medical anthropologist Charles Briggs candidly explained how scholarship often develops. "One of my defense mechanisms," he wrote, "is turning issues that trouble me into research projects" (2007, 315). This is a sentiment that resonates strongly with Brigittine, who reflected on her research in a similar fashion:

> Many, if not all, of my research projects have emerged out of a persistent question regarding some form of what I understood to be violence or exclusion that started as a recurring concern, irritation, and sometimes even outrage in my own mind. I generally don't plan research questions in the very initial phase of work; I encounter them organically as troubling or disturbing social, political, and/or scholarly facts around me. I then start looking for analytic and empirical tools to engage them.

Overall in this chapter, we see threads of anthropological passions and challenges centered more on questions concerning them, or engaging with them, rather than on finding definitive answers to them. We share these motivations ourselves, but here we want to share other anthropologists' passions as well.

Passions

Carolyn Sargent's earliest passions had nothing to do with anthropology, but she did see a strong link between them in retrospect:

My lifelong passions are piano, detective fiction, and various aspects of medicine: history of medicine, culture of medicine, and all the other sorts of things that medical anthropologists get involved with. Nobody's going to pay me for reading detective fiction, I'm afraid. Piano's my first love, and I have a picture of myself at the age of two with a large bow in my hair and many curls sitting at a grand piano, and looking sort of like [Vladimir] Horowitz or Arthur Rubinstein with my hands in the air about to make a crashing sound. So piano was really the most important thing to me until I was about sixteen or seventeen, really until I went to college. I think there's some sort of inverse relationship between how shy I was and how embedded in piano I was and then as I went through high school and became a little less shy.

Then I had a social network that I was much more involved with. I was into Russian novels, so it was Chopin, Rachmaninoff, and Dostoyevsky. You can see that I had a dramatic interior life. I started as a teenager with Agatha Christie, which is pure comfort reading that you can read over and over again, and I do feel that Miss Marple—one of Agatha Christie's most famous heroines—has influenced my anthropological work. . . . Miss Marple is fond of thinking of her villain—[in] St. Mary Mead and wherever she is—and thinking up the chemist's boy, who seemed like he was a nice boy but actually was doing nasty experiments in the backroom. You know, it's been solving a mystery by relating it to personal biographies and experiences she had, friendships she was aware of, and so forth. I think a sense of what communities and networks are like. . . . Miss Marple's perspective on evil, because Agatha Christie was writing at a time when there was a lot of debate about whether wickedness, as she called it, was actually genetic and criminals could be excused for their crimes because it was somehow an inherited quality. She always said, "No, there really is evil and there really is wickedness in the world."

When given the opportunity to reflect on their passions, several anthropologists across the four fields turned eagerly toward their specific research interests and questions that have been professional lifelong commitments and joys. These brief excerpts give a sense of the astonishing range of passions that compel particular anthropologists.

Leslie C. Aiello told Virginia,

When you actually think of it, the Upper Paleolithic in the South of France, after the last glacial advance, was pretty much close to a paradigm. . . . There were still large herd animals. It was probably a situation quite similar to the Northwest Coast, where you could have hunting-and-gathering people that were quite stationary and, of course, you had the wonderful artistic tradition of the cave art. . . . The whole point is that modern society is a very, very recent thing and all you have to do is look at the charts of increase of human population and realize the impact of the Industrial Revolution and realize that the way we live today is not the way that we lived in most of our evolutionary history, and that's one of the exciting things of understanding what the alternative of the modern day is and the past was and how it has changed, why it has changed, and try to project what they have into the future.

Agustín Fuentes said,

Macaques—monkeys—fascinate me for a number of reasons, but some of those reasons are the same reasons people fascinate me. I know that is a little facile, but let me explain. I've worked with a wide variety. I've worked with apes, I've worked with a different number of primate species, and I've obviously worked with humans and with some nonprimate animals as well. But macaques and humans share some very interesting patterns. We both have this radical expansion about two million years ago in the Pleistocene. We have the two most successful primate genera, *Homo* and macaque. We live across the widest array of habitats, and we are also the two primate species that probably get along better than any other. At least macaques and humans get together more than humans and any other primate and any other large-body mammal. That's one of the interests. The other thing is that they have these very large, complex social groups where males and females and their offspring and their distant relatives sort of live together in very complex and day-to-day social relationships. Once studying nonhuman organisms, I am drawn to the fact that they have that complexity of sociality because one of my big interests is where does sociality come from and especially where do the complex intersocial divisions emerge. I think the comparative context [is good], to understand primates in general, but also to maybe think about human uniqueness.

These three anthropologists have enduring passions for big questions about the nature of the human condition over time. Marilyn Strathern turned our attention in a different direction linked to a concern with humanity in a particular place and time:

I was trying to think of how one might think of passion as something that one's passionate about, and there is no doubt that Melanesia's got under my skin. Mind you, of course, it's "Melanesia" in quotation marks. It's not an issue that

I've, I'm not going to say helped create—I'm not Malinowski[1]—but that has filtered through the way I've been thinking about it for a long time. So it's a little indulgent as well, in that sense. What, in fact, gives me huge pleasure is when, occasionally, I get confirmation from a Papua New Guinean scholar, or from people over there, that actually what I think of sort of [as] my flights of fancy are actually a bit more grounded than I might otherwise think. And that's been very rewarding. But there's no doubt that I'm in one of my happiest states when I'm dealing with ethnographic materials from that part of the world.

Here we see both satisfaction and humility, and anthropologists often exhibit these emotions when they talk about what they try to do and why. Consider the following perspectives that highlight the relevance of theory to everyday lives, emergent social phenomena, and matters of evidence.

Jacqueline Comito told Brigittine,

To me [it's] that the most exciting theoretical frameworks were coming out of linguistic anthropology, the language and culture, the performance-based stuff, the semiotics, oh my gosh. But it's not so far off from what I used to do with dramatic interpretation from literature. It's the same. It's like literary analysis but not something that somebody actually made up. In this case you're looking at it; it's actually happening. And, you know, Goffman was another one I thought. He did *The Presentation of Self in Everyday Life* [Goffman 1959].[2] Just read that, and if that doesn't change your life, what would!

Tom Boellstorff told Virginia,

In terms of what I've loved about *Second Life*,[3] I hardly get to go into it right now because of the editorship [of *American Anthropologist*] and teaching and everything else, which has been fab for me because I knew when I became an editor that there would be a price to pay that way. But, you know, for me, I mean I was lucky that I began my research when *Second Life* was very new and

---

[1] Bronislaw Malinowski (1884–1942) is considered one of the founders of the discipline of anthropology internationally. He was Polish by birth but claimed by the British social anthropologists as a founder of their field. He is typically thought of as having set a disciplinary standard of long-term, hands-on fieldwork. Much of the work he did in the South Pacific during World War I is often now considered distant and unethical, but he is still typically seen as one of the key founders of modern social anthropology.

[2] Erving Goffman (1922–1982) was a Canadian sociologist long read and used in linguistic and sociocultural anthropology.

[3] *Second Life* is an online game that Tom played for several years. He also wrote a book about it that is also about doing anthropological fieldwork.

very small, and it's been fascinating to watch a new set of communities and social norms come into being and grow and expand and—and now there's so many different kinds of virtual worlds and also social networking sites like Facebook—that to sort of watch an emergence of culture taking form has been very interesting to me and to sort of see the incredible, you know—people talk about deception and mean stuff that people do online and can be there but, you know, 90 percent or more of what happens is incredible kindness—people taking the time to show you things and people being incredible friends to each other and doing incredibly creative work together. That's been really fascinating to explore and see what it is that people are doing and, you know, for myself, to discover a love of building inside of *Second Life* and building a house and building things with people and just an array of things that whenever you do ethnography you are finding things that you never knew that you would find and I've just been very pleased by that. It's been very, very wonderful.

Virginia observed,

I actually worry about matters of evidence. I want people to think, to have imagination, to think about contributing at a theoretical level. But I really want them to be asking questions that are manageable, so how you relate that to theory is a matter of evidence. I worry about people who have overly small questions even though they can do good things with them, and then I worry a great deal about people who ask really big questions and can't quite relate them to a particular topic, so it's really one of my passions. We have to go for that middle range.

Notice that enthusiasm and commitment are clearly present in all of the foregoing perspectives, but also note the way anthropologists pull back, relate to others, and seek reasonable, believable statements and claims. From this professional orientation, passions are often things to be explored, tested, and checked out with care over long periods of time.

In addition to deep passions for a variety of particular research inquiries, topics, and themes, this group of accomplished anthropologists also expressed great passion for and profound enjoyment of reading and writing as personal and professional activities both inside and outside the academy. As we will see, reading and writing cross genres, forms, and audiences.

Jeremy Arac Sabloff observed,

Another [passion] which I think all of us have to have as scholars is reading. And one of the hardest things when you become an administrator is finding the time to do general reading, and I have to begrudge every minute I have to read more broadly, not just in anthropology but in the sciences. I would love to have time to read mysteries and science fiction, which I enjoy immensely. I think the difference in my life today [from my life] twenty years ago [is that then] I could read a novel a night and go to sleep at two o'clock in the morning and wake up at a reasonable hour and function. Now I find by eleven o'clock I'm falling asleep with the book on my chest.

Here is Carolyn again:

One [passion] is continuing with the Basker Prize Committee.[4] That prize, as you know—and probably everyone knows—is for an outstanding book or work on gender and health, and I've really enjoyed being on that committee with you [Virginia] and whatever other committee member has participated over the years and it's an opportunity to read a selection of works on what is my own research area. So in a sense I have more time to read thoughtfully and carefully and to enjoy the array of books that we get to review.

On the subject of reading and writing, João Biehl stated,

I love to hear what a book does to the reader. And in some ways, I take this as the formative potential of anthropology and of writing—to generate a reading and open up for both the writer and the reader something that has been known before. I love what you [Virginia] said about getting close to people and being intimate with them without patronizing them or assuming [anything about them], and I, in some ways, did it when I did the work with Catarina and I wrote *Vita* [Biehl 2005]. . . . I thought I had to give all I had. And this *Vita* was the book that I actually wanted to write. Everything that I ever learned or experienced had to be implied to try to understand this one human life.

I like to think that it is one of the possibilities and the strengths of anthropology as knowledge making, to get close to people in their complexity and afford them some of the same ambiguities and complexities that we afford ourselves and then find a way to represent them that does not necessarily turn them into caricatures or into just, how can I say it, into illustrations of prior assumptions or philosophical thought as beautiful or concepts as beautiful as they might sound or be. And Catarina was quite powerful in that regard because when I began working with her, then she asked me to come and listen

[4] The Eileen Basker Memorial Prize was established in 1987 and is run by the Society for Medical Anthropology. It is often given to a book by a medical anthropologist, but it is open to works by authors in all disciplines and of all nationalities and has so far been given to works by sociologists, historians, and nursing scholars and to works by colleagues in at least five different countries.

to her so there was something that she put into me and there was something very powerful. It was like a life force there. It was something that I think is very underreflected upon in this power of sublimation on how people are able to transcend their conditions and do something else with whatever their lives have become. I think that this is a very difficult ethical position, but I think it is also one that we, as anthropologists, contribute to understanding.

On the more personal front, I yearn to write a child's story. Fiction. I yearn for that. I love telling stories to my son, Andre.

Jeremy said,

I actually enjoy writing. And I think I am passionate. I find writing quite exciting and absorbing. I should say that I still write on a yellow pad as I have since my graduate student days. Now the second step is going from the yellow pad onto my computer but, in fact, it gives me an extra stage of editing. I also like to write where there is a lot of noise and other activities going on around me. My favorite place to write is watching sports on TV. I sit on a chair and a couch with my yellow pad. I used to joke that one of the sad developments that's hurt writing is the instant replay. Because football was great. I would watch a play and forty-five seconds later I would sit and scribble, and now my thing is to catch the instant replay. I do better at halftime than I do when it is going on. I love college basketball, and I always used to go to that with a pad and write at halftime.

Some of these statements might be surprising. Jeremy writing while watching sports? João struggling to figure out how to write about Catarina? Carolyn being happy to serve on a committee because she gets to read? And yet these are all things very successful anthropologists have told us about their perhaps unexpected experiences reading and writing and their passions surrounding those practices.

Clearly, for some anthropologists working inside the academy, teaching and working with students is a particular joy and passion that makes an anthropological life quite rewarding. Most anthropologists experience this not instead of doing research but rather in tandem with it. Tom, for example, told Virginia,

Compared to a lot of jobs out there, and having worked other jobs before academia, I just think [that] to be able to teach and do research is such an honor and such a joy.

And João expressed his love for teaching as well:

I also want to continue one of the things that I love the most about my work—teaching. I think teaching is my vocation. I think that as anthropologists we do incredible public service by the kind of evidence and work that we publish but also in teaching. And that is related to your last question, to what has moved me so much.

Brigittine details what she loves about teaching:

For me, working with students, both teaching in the classroom and individual mentoring, is a constant source of joy. Most days, teaching really bright, engaged, eager, and critical young people is a true pleasure. It is a good challenge to find new ways and translatable ways of explaining anthropological ideas like symbolic violence, or how language is a form of action, or how something like individual memory can have a collective component. These pedagogical practices make me a better scholar and a better listener. I love giving students, both undergraduates and graduates, in different ways, the tools to make their own knowledge in the world, and to use it in ways that they find compelling and important. I feel honored to help my students find their own voices and passions.

For these anthropologists, teaching is way of serving the public and, in turn, empowering individuals to change the world.

Anthropology and Public Engagement

Passions take many forms, and one of them for many anthropologists is engaging with the public, affecting public opinion, and even changing public policy. We do not just mean the public within universities and colleges. Anthropologists' engagement with the public beyond the academy is a profoundly important issue for the discipline and for many of its practitioners. For some, it is a deep commitment; for others, it is a practice to be admired, a source of inspiration, and also a major worry. The multifaceted place of anthropology's participation in public life is an enduring issue that has spurred ethical, personal, intellectual, political, and professional concerns since the formalization of the field well into the twenty-first century. Former American Anthropological Association president Leith Mullings reflects on the history of anthropological engagement with pressing social issues in her discussion of why anthropology matters:

As the post–World War II consequences of racism became all too clear in the face of the challenges raised by the black freedom struggle and the wars of liberation, several anthropologists, in particular Franz Boas and his students—including Ashley Montagu, Ruth Benedict, and Gene Weltfish,[5] among others—actively participated in shaping public views about race. Though most accepted the validity of some version of the race concept, they worked for racial justice. Boas developed a long-term collaboration with civil rights activist and sociologist W. E. B. Du Bois and other members of the NAACP. Others were deeply involved in developing the 1950 UNESCO document, *The Race Question*. In working to disavow popular concepts of race and racial hierarchies, they were later joined by biological anthropologists such as Sherwood Washburn and Frank Livingstone. Stimulated by antiracist struggles, these new anthropological perspectives about race in turn supported the work of activists, most notably in public school desegregation cases. (2015, 6)

This long-term disciplinary engagement with broader public issues has not produced a single experience or position that encapsulates the complexities, desires, and frustrations associated with anthropological engagement in the social world today. Instead, here we see a sampling of multiple ways that anthropologists put their discipline to work in the public sphere beyond the field itself. Public dissemination in media, policy efforts, activism, and advocacy are all rich venues in which anthropologists have practiced and continue to practice with varying degrees of satisfaction.

Lee D. Baker highlighted the long-standing engagement with the public in the life of Boas that Mullings foregrounded. To Virginia, he said,

I admire [Boas] for the time. I mean, he was much more naive than what I think people give him credit [for]. He was savvy on some things but kind of naive on others. He was brave, nevertheless. Maybe his naïveté enabled him to be braver than he would have been otherwise. So I admire his commitment to bringing anthropology into the public sphere. I admire that.

---

[5] Ashley Montagu (1905–1999) was a biological anthropologist who was well known for critiquing the U.S. public's idea of race.

Ruth Benedict (1887–1948) was one of the most influential U.S. anthropologists of the first half of the twentieth century, one of Franz Boas's most famous students, and a leader in what was long known as "the culture and personality school." She is best known for her books *Patterns of Culture* (published in 1934) and *The Chrysanthemum and the Sword* (published in 1946).

Gene Weltfish (1902–1980) was a U.S. anthropologist and historian working at Columbia University from 1928 to 1953. A former student of Franz Boas, she focused on the culture and history of the Pawnee people of the Midwest Plains. She is also well known as coauthor, with Ruth Benedict, of the 1943 pamphlet *The Races of Mankind*, which she and Benedict wrote for the U.S. Army during World War II.

Other anthropologists explain their own complicated and long-standing efforts to use anthropological work to influence social issues they care about deeply. Notice the struggles but also the passions our colleagues describe. Carolyn Sargent said,

Some of the questions that I raised [as president of the Society for Medical Anthropology], at least one of them, was what can anthropologists do to contribute to this debate and also if there's some kind of infrastructure that we could create where we could funnel relevant research to policy makers since we have lots of research obviously. It's not clear that very many policy makers ever read it. So, with that in mind, based on responses I got from colleagues who heard my talk or read my article in the *MAQ* [*Medical Anthropology Quarterly*] that was based on my talk, I put together a task force.

I recently moved to Wash U [Washington University] in Saint Louis, and we have a very generous new dean, Gary Will, who decided that he would support a meeting of the task force at Wash U. Last month we had a meeting here for three days, or two and a half days, with about a dozen people, and we brainstormed about these various issues having to do with roles for anthropologists, medical anthropologists, economic anthropologists, and so forth. And one of the things that came up was that perhaps we might want to talk to some legislators about what they needed, if anything. And we had some of our colleagues with connections to legislators or family members who are legislators, so we all checked with whoever in our personal networks might be useful. My colleague Pete Benson, also at Wash U, and I were invited by Russ Carnahan, who is the representative of our area of Missouri to the U.S. Congress, to come to Washington and meet with him and talk about what our plans were, and I think this is because Washington University is his constituent.

Pete and I went off to Washington not exactly sure what we were doing, but it was really fascinating, and it gave us a lot of ideas. Representative Carnahan was kind enough to take time from a foreign relations committee meeting that he was supposed to be at (so his assistant kept looking at her watch and making faces at him over Pete's head), but he kept talking to us, which was very nice. I would say—to summarize what he and others of his colleagues said to us—that they have mountains of literature that land on their desks. The question is who reads it, if anyone reads it, and whether it's ever translated into any kind of policy. I think that the answer to that is not as much we probably would like.

Part of the issue, not surprisingly, is that a lot of the materials that they get are in book form or article form and nobody has time to read it. So we talked to him about whether it would be useful to have digests or bullet points or some kind of annotated bibliographies of work that anthropologists had done. And he thought that was a great idea. It occurred to Pete and me that groups like the Medical Anthropology Student Association—the graduate student association—might be interested in participating and coming up with those sorts of digests. So that was one idea and the other was one that Rep. Carnahan became rather animated about—the idea that if he or some of the other legislators or their staff had a question about the impact of forthcoming legislation on their constituents, they could ask anthropologists, they could target that issue and come up with a response. . . . So it would be sort of research on demand.

Tom stated,

Advocacy and activist work are extremely important and, to me, there's no contradiction. So especially in my Indonesia work with gay and lesbian and transgender Indonesians, my ethnographic practice. I just don't know what I would do all day if I wasn't working with these gay NGOs and writing grants for them and helping them in all kinds of ways. It gives me something to do. It gives me a sort of sense of access. It gives me something to give back, and it just gives me something to do. I mean, because I thought always doing interviewing and doing participant observation through the NGOs is just such an awesome way to do it.

I couldn't have done what I've done otherwise, and so, to me, the theoretical, intellectual work that I've done in my Indonesia work is completely fused with the activist work and there's no contradiction whatsoever because I sort of came out of AIDS NGO, nongovernmental organization, work into that Indonesia work in the first place. I used to work in an organization called the Institute for Community Health Outreach in San Francisco that trains outreach workers, and I sort of got started by having gained those skills there. I became a sort of consultant, going to Russia and to Malaysia, to Indonesia, sort of helping NGOs set up street outreach programs, and that's sort of how I got into these spaces. I was a consultant doing HIV/AIDS work [and] I still do to this day. So that said, you know, around the value of intellectual work, activist work, I think, is an extremely important and useful tool, and there needs to be no conflict whatsoever with intellectual work.

We think this is very much the case for Nandini Sundar, too. Notice what she told Virginia:

I've been passionate about this litigation that I've been involved in for the people that I work with—on behalf of the people I did fieldwork with—and the reason why is something that sort of borders on an obsession. It is because the kind of selflessness that is involved has been quite different. I don't mean selflessness, but it's a way of having to sort of subordinate every other thing to the sort of logic of the litigation and the logic of the campaign against the counterinsurgency that's been going on.

Let me just give you a little background. I started to work in central India among Indigenous people in the early nineties, and in mid-2005 the government started to pay attention. This area has seen a lot of mobilization by Maoist guerillas over the last thirty years, people who are now effectively in control of large areas. So in 2005 the government started a counterinsurgency campaign which involved a combination of strategic actions of vigilante groups or civil patrols which went on burning villages and killing people. People were forced into camps. I had actually stopped working on this area for quite a while in between but, when this happened, I went back, and it was just the most horrible thing that I've seen. So I began to campaign against it and also then in 2007 filed a lawsuit in the Supreme Court [of India]. Unlike everything else, once it comes to litigation in the courts, it's impossible to dictate one's own time or to dictate even the kind of testimonies that one submits in court. These are a sort of complex combination of what you actually want to say yourself and what the court requires, so I've had to be somebody that I'm not necessarily. In a way, I've had to give up my academic freedom to say what I want to say, to say things that need to be said in a particular legal fashion.

Overall, these professional experiences and perspectives support Jeremy Arac Sabloff's assessment of anthropologists' public engagement when he claimed,

I've seen many more successful attempts than unsuccessful ones—at least of those I'm aware have been unsuccessful. I think I may be more optimistic than others. I recognize that there are significant hurdles in terms of broad public outreach, but given the kind of progress you've seen in recent years, I'm at least guardedly optimistic.

Despite these anthropologists' multiple and layered successes with anthropological engagement in public debates, activism, and advocacy, other anthropologists identified these areas as profound concerns and challenges for their professional lives. In other words, these anthropologists viewed the challenges of public engagement to be great and successes elusive.

Virginia said,

The usual thing that I hear from colleagues is that I tried here and there. But the truth is that they haven't gotten very far. They have written pieces for magazines or op-eds and these haven't been picked up. Or they have tried to talk to some broad audience in some interview and only the very basic ideas get picked up and were, in any case, misunderstood. You know what I mean? There is a sense that they try and, somehow, we are not listened to much. The problem is that comments like that can become both depressing and maybe a little bit condescending towards the general public. I don't think this attitude helps us.

Agustín Fuentes stated,

It does [make me mad]. If you go back to the sixties and even seventies, anthropologists still had a prominent place in the public eye, I think. Not a lot but enough and also major statements by someone like Ashley Montagu or Margaret Mead or Clifford Geertz.[6] These made the *New York Times*. They were major, at least in this literary or cultural world in the United States. They made an impact. This is still true to a certain extent in parts of Europe. But today in the United States it is very difficult for anthropology to demonstrate its worth. Not to ourselves and not in our research but very much in the public arena. I don't think there are enough anthropologists spending enough time writing op-eds, making loud public gestures, or giving public speeches.

Jeremy stated,

I'm going to argue about this need [for more public engagement].[7] I know there won't be people who necessarily agree. I think right now we need a lot more Margaret Meads, and I was going to talk about what we can do to make that possible.

Leslie C. Aiello observed,

[Public engagement] is a huge problem. And it's not knowing how to go about doing it to make a significant difference. Certainly getting anthropology out there is of most importance, whether it's through op-eds in the newspapers or by other means. It's why when I visit the UK I used to do a lot of BBC work, and it's just to try to get anthropology into the popular media so people were aware of it and can become excited about it. . . . I think it's a responsibility that we all should think about—how we could popularize more of our research and what, for example, we've done for *Current Anthropology*.[8] We're starting to issue press releases to some of the papers that we think may have a broader

[6] Margaret Mead (1901–1978) did much of her anthropological fieldwork in Samoa but in her middle age and later years devoted much time to commenting publicly on the contemporary United States. Clifford Geertz (1926–2006), who was trained as a Southeast Asianist and wrote his earliest books about agriculture and trading in Indonesia, went on to become extremely well known for his humanistic, interpretive notion of culture.
[7] See Sabloff (2011). An anthropological archaeologist, Jeremy has long been interested in anthropologists being a large part of public discussion, and this article of his is just one example.
[8] *Current Anthropology* is an international journal of anthropology, long supported financially and intellectually by the Wenner-Gren Foundation for Anthropological Research and published by the University of Chicago Press.

impact and those are being picked up in the media. That small thing with the [Wenner-Gren] Foundation website, we are going to be stepping into social media and we're hoping we can highlight much more the results of the research of our grantees.

Here is an exchange between Agustín and Virginia about relationships between scholarship and public engagement. In the former, anthropologists have much more control than in the latter. Agustín puts it well when he says,

I know many of us are out trying to get it [anthropological work] out beyond the confines of our published words and the academy, and, you're right, there is a hierarchy of access, but part of that hierarchy of access is filtered through a kind of public presentation of self. Many professors, for example, are hesitant to jump into the public frame, and I don't have an answer to it, but there has to be a way to get out there with short, coherent sound bites that also contain the kind of quality we seek in the kind of discussion we want to present. I think it is difficult to crack, but I think it's possible. One way to do it is to put yourself out there more and more, even though it may lead to very embarrassing moments.

I work with the press whenever I can, even though I would say more than 50 percent of the time I'm not happy with the outcome, but you have to learn how to interact and you also have to learn to speak across generations and across backgrounds to access them. If you watch any basic media available on television or the internet, the ways in which information is presented are relatively alien to most academics. I don't know if I'm comfortable with it. I just know it's important, so I think part of it is trying to negotiate that.

I recently did a piece on Animal Planet Channel that I'm not super happy about. It's called *Untamed and Uncut*, and . . . I got about eight minutes in it or something like that. It was an interview. It was about a family in Bali that got bitten by a monkey in one of these monkey parks, where I've done this type of research, so they asked me to sort of narrate what is happening. The bottom line is . . . that people need to learn how to interact, perhaps especially how if you're not from that area, how to minimize the rule of conflict between tourists and monkeys, and how you can have an enjoyable and safe experience when going on these visits. But the way in which the Animal Planet producers edited it was with dramatic music, and some of the camera angles were not my choice, so you get this "when monkeys attack" motif going on. But at the same time, people have watched that and people come up to me at airports and say, "Oh you're the guy on this and that," and we engage in discussions. People email me and they do get some of the bottom line. I'm not saying it's the right way to do it, but sometimes we have to figure out how to get our ideas and thoughts out there.

Virginia asked,

Is some of this compromising either our positions or the way we package them so that we have a chance of getting some of the message out there? You're saying that you can't even choose the framing?

Agustín responded,

I did not [choose the framing]. And they didn't cut out much of what I said, so I would not compromise, if it was something and they showed it to me. I would not compromise. I would not allow something that I was in to go public if I could help it and if it was incorrect or misrepresentative. But at the same time, it was definitely the kind of package that I would not have used. So I compromised the packaging, but I think the content went out well. And that's a hard call and I don't know exactly what to do about it. I don't think there is a guidebook for that call. I think it is something we might consider doing more often.

Virginia observed,

I just don't altogether know to what extent it is partially what anthropologists are, or are not doing, on the one hand, and what is going on elsewhere out there that makes it hard for people to think of us as having things to contribute beyond what they anticipate, and often what they anticipate is that we are experts on very interesting cultures of the world that have either largely died out or live very far away.

Alaka Wali clearly thinks about public engagement all the time, both what works and what does not work. To Virginia, she said,

They talk about engaged universities nowadays. There is a lot of talk about that, but we are still mired in a system of promotion and tenure and thinking about universities that does not make engagement very easy. In fact, it makes it diffi-cult.... [Museum are] absolutely more open to that. I think there is a lot more experience now, experience as engaged work here as museums. I think the kind of people who come to work in museum settings are committed to that. Even (and I must say "even") my colleagues who are archaeologists are setting up small museums in the communities where they are doing their research. They are much more fluid on how they think about that. We love talking to public audiences.

We [in museums] also do, and participate in, exhibits of major areas of the world. Look at the new hall of the ancient Americas[9] at the Field Museum. It

_____

[9] The Field Museum has been redoing many of its exhibits over the past few decades. The museum itself was first established in connection with the 1893 Chicago World's Fair and used to be called the Field Museum of Natural History. Many of the exhibits now being

took a lot of territorial ties to redo that hall. But, you know, this is what we're committed to do with the million visitors who will go through that hall in a year. This is a huge impact you can have, and I think when you have that ability to be engaged with the public in different kinds of ways and with different publics, you should do so. I think that is a big difference. It is not that scholars in universities aren't also wanting to be engaged, but I think the structure of the university makes it more difficult.

Alaka is right about large museums having a bigger public than most universities and colleges, but it is interesting, too, that in the last few years, at least in the United States, many universities and colleges have started requiring faculty members to do "outreach," sometimes even called "public engagement." Some anthropologists have always done it, because of the typical anthropological goal of affecting public opinion, but some, like João, actually talk about it, even in the context of a privileged academic position:

I get a lot of questions from my students about how to transform this [anthropological understanding] into policy. I get these technocratic and normative questions. And I just tell them it's up to you guys. We can produce a certain kind of evidence and I think the burden should not be on us to now make the policy, but we now have to find the ways to communicate our findings to a broader public. And we have to be more ingenious and creative—finding alternative forms and genres to express what we find. We should not just settle for books, which might take five to ten years to do, or just for a peer-reviewed article in a professional journal. There are other forms in which we should participate and enlarge public debate. There is nothing more important than bringing people into public debate and talking about interventions and public policies.

While all these anthropologists view public engagement as a major priority for the discipline and its practitioners, there is no clear or set path for doing so. Anthropologists are challenged by a lack of training in how to engage meaningfully, and they are frustrated by the transformation of nuanced anthropological understandings into ideas and representations that may simplify too much. There are now more and more graduate programs in anthropology in the United States that talk about engaged anthropology and some that train anthropologists to do that work, but many anthropologists still feel they do not do enough of it, especially as they tend to want to do more and more of it throughout their careers.

---

changed reflected views from the early twentieth century, which are often seriously out of date and do not conform to contemporary anthropological understandings.

Frustrations and Challenges

In addition to these ongoing concerns and challenges for efficacious anthropological involvement with the public, anthropologists expressed frustration with disciplinary tensions around the four fields, ongoing social injustice, and forms of inequality in the contemporary world. Some of those who identify as women highlighted these issues through a particular gendered frame in the professional sphere, and we want to make sure to include those observations here, but we also want readers to notice the kinds of interventions these colleagues make as a way of confronting these challenges, and we want readers to think of some men, maybe male-identified anthropologists, as very much aware of gender. Jacqueline Comito, for example, told Brigittine,

> It is a challenge to be an anthropologist in this [field of agriculture], too, because half the time nobody understands what I'm trying to do and I'm training people because I can't hire a bunch of anthropologists. I have to take other people. I have to help them with content background, too. So I have to train people to be able to do some of these methods, you know. Getting people to think a little bit differently is a huge challenge. But I think it's important because I've been impacted so much more as a result of it.

Agustín observed,

> I think my biggest complaint about anthropology is that not enough effort is put forward by anthropologists to work together or to work across other disciplines to really maximize the capacity that we can have. . . . I think there is a dual problem. There is a historical problem where there is a pretty significant and long-lasting rift that emerged in the eighties, and there were a lot of bad feelings and a lot of anger in multiple directions. Some of it is valid and some of it is not valid. I think we're in the process of moving past that. Again, when people say four fields, I think, well, fine, whatever. Four fields, five fields, I don't really care. What I really care about are questions and what we do to deploy, to answer, questions, and for me it is the methodologies and training. So I say that I am an anthropologist. I'm a biological anthropologist, which means that most of my interests revolve around areas where a biological tool kit is of great relevance. That does not mean that all anthropologists have to have that by any stretch of the imagination, but more biological anthropologists should be in the AAA [American Anthropological Association]. However, more sociocultural anthropologists need to develop a greater appreciation for biological anthropology. I think it is a two-way street.

Alaka stated,

I was queasy about coming to the Field Museum. I think, you know, I have written about the fact that I came into anthropology at this moment in the 1970s when we were all about decolonizing anthropology and making anthropology work for social change and coming to institutions with deep roots in colonialist practice and history and that represent and maximize some things to many of us in this generation of anthropologists. It was a queasy feeling. But, as you know, I struggle with that or have thought about it. I have thought about what we can do to change that, and to use the institution and have some impact different from what its history was.

Because any of these institutions, you know, what are you going to do with them? Either they sit here and fossilize, no pun [intended, or we do something about them]. . . . We have a collection of over a million objects. Are we going to repatriate all those objects? We cannot because the people often do not know whose heritage it was. They may not have the resources to take care of them, nor do I necessarily think that that would be the best thing to do with these objects or collections. So . . . do we just keep them in storage and only let scholars look at them? It is a dilemma, and I think people in the museum community, also in the 1980s and 1990s, were thinking about these dilemmas and started to write about how museums have to be transformed. That has been a huge challenge, I think, for those that do work in these institutions. They/we need to be critical, and there is a lot of critique of museum practice in anthropology that is very insightful. But then those of us who work here [at the Field Museum] have to go beyond critique and think about what we are going to do. If we are here and we are going to take it seriously, then what? That's where I have tried to focus my efforts. I have no doubt that it is a colonialist institution, [and] that it has problematic pasts, and very problematic representations of peoples, not just Indigenous peoples.

Notice that Agustín is primarily concerned with fragmentation within the profession of anthropology, while Jacqueline and Alaka are challenged by the people they work with, the objects they work with, the institutions that employ them, and the ways they might be able to change them. But all anthropologists share a passion for noticing inequalities and figuring out some ways they could ameliorate them. Their employers vary, their areas of work vary, their interventions vary, and their strategies vary, but in all there is as much passion as there is frustration that strengthens that passion.

Notice what Monica Heller told Virginia in her interview (and this is something important enough to us to repeat here):

What I have certainly gotten sort of obsessed about most of my career has been issues around the ways in which problems of social difference and social inequality get played out on the terrain of language. Well, I mean, that's sort of the central thing that I keep worrying about all the time, and not just in my work but also in many aspects of my life. I guess I don't make a very clear distinction necessarily between what I consider to be work and the rest of my life, and I suppose that it's one of [those] classic problems of trying to understand how societies work. Why do we have these categories? Why do we have these forms of social difference, and how come they get used to make relations of power? Growing up in Canada, growing up in Montreal, the stuff has all been—and is still in many respects—played out as a language issue, although it's not always clear to me that it centrally is language. It may be forms of essentially class inequality that get constructed in linguistic terms.

Tom Boellstorff stated,

That's really what I said there about [what makes me sad and mad]—talent, especially about injustice, talent wasted, and lives cut short. You know I've done that work since 1990 now, so it's really twenty years since I was in college. I've been doing work with HIV/AIDS, and that is exciting, inspirational work, but it's really hard because I have so many friends who've died. I've seen them die with horrible diseases that could have been prevented and treated better and I've had to go to the friend's place, the house of friends who were dying of AIDS, in Indonesia with literally nothing but aspirin in my hand and just feeling like a complete idiot because in this particular city, in this particular year, that's all we had. One case was before the antiretroviral drugs were available in Sulawesi. I hated to see a beautiful person die, or within a few weeks of dying, of a disease that we knew how to stop, that we could have stopped. No one should be dying of AIDS or getting infected with HIV in the year 2011. It shouldn't have been happening in the year 2001 or the year 1991.

Very soon after the epidemic began, we knew how to prevent almost all infections—condoms and needles and blood testing. We could have HIV almost completely wiped out through really simple technologies. But, because of stigma and injustice, it's still happening, and people think there's a cure or whatever, and it's in some ways worse than it was before. So it's really hard to see friends of mine get infected with HIV and see them die and, you know, it is also inspiring to see them fight and live healthy, good lives, and so it's not all bad. But it's a hard thing to see it happen, and so it does make me sad and mad to see people getting infected when there's no excuse, no reason that people— so many people—should be getting HIV in this day and age. It's actually a hard virus to get. It's a lot harder to get than a cold or even hepatitis. It's a fragile virus. There's only a couple of ways to transmit it, and there's no reason that people should still be getting infected. It's just really unjust that that is still happening.

Virginia also asked interviewees what makes them mad or sad, and many conveyed both passion and frustration in their responses. Monica, for example, told Virginia that she does not "like things that are secretive" and that instead she likes "things to be transparent and explicit and direct. So anything that feels kind of hidden and mystified in some way does make [her] crazy." And Carolyn Sargent responded with a lengthy statement about unfairness:

> What makes me mad? Things that are unfair and people who seem to me to be hypocritical. I have a very low tolerance of situations that seem to me to be unjust, which has sometimes gotten me in trouble in my professional life.... There was a time at SMU [Southern Methodist University] when there wasn't a deadline for letting people know if they were going to receive tenure, and there were various people who suffered a great deal from not having a decision and just living in uncertainty for what I thought was an unacceptably long time. So I tackled some administrators on trying to change the rules and eventually we did have some regulations in place as to how long after the department met, after the deans committee met, after the provost committee met, did one have to be informed of the results of that meeting.

This affected all faculty members who were considered for promotion at SMU, but Carolyn was also very aware of the ways it affected women faculty members seeking promotion.

Here are other statements made by anthropologists discussing their personal experiences with gender disparity in their professional lives both in and outside the academy, and what they have done about them. Jacqueline explained,

> It's also not easy to be a female working in agriculture and working in an extension project. This issue of gender and academia particularly I would state [is a challenge], but I think every place has these challenges, and the current movement right now, like the #metoo movement, clearly stresses the relevance of gender. I am fortunate. I have never truly had what I would consider sexual harassment or not even anything that I would say would even get close to that, but I have had moments where I have been treated in a certain way that, if I were male, I would not have been treated, or judged in a certain way, particularly as a supervisor.
>
> I bring this up and it's funny because everyone will deny it, like when I point out to Human Resources, "You know this is kind of an issue. It's hard to be a female supervisor." It's very difficult because, like, I might be demanding and I could be, I am demanding and I'm very driven and, you know, with women that gets presented in a different way. I get judged a lot more for it. I'm also Italian American and that gets expressed in certain ways. I've been told—and I'm still being told—that I'm not behaving the right way as an Iowan.

Carolyn observed,

A lot of what I did in Women's Studies [at SMU] had to do with salary inequities. I suppose I was fortunate, although the president of SMU later said to me that it was a pity that being on the gender equity salary committee was as upsetting to me as it was. I sure wanted to stay on it, and his was not the ideal response. I would have liked him to say, "Well, since you found all these inequities, we will fix them," instead of saying, "Well, perhaps you'd like to leave this committee since it upsets you." But there was a particular provost at SMU who decided he wanted to do a salary equity study and asked the commission on the status of women, which I was then chair of, or cochair of, to do this. He gave us all the raw data by department and year of rank, and we did a really accurate analysis of salaries and gender and race. We found a lot of inequities, and I think about fifteen or twenty people had immediate remedial major raises. And then several of us got letters saying we had been systematically underpaid since hiring, and that's the kind of thing that made me extremely mad.

Monica stated,

A feeling that I certainly have as a member of my generation, that I see my daughter's generation going through also, is that it's still difficult, you know, for women. Despite all the progress that has been made for women, and for all kinds of marginalized groups, you still—you know—they still got to fight really, really, really hard. There's still a lot of gender discrimination. I mean this kind of blithe domination that I was talking about earlier that reproduces that marginalization. Stuff that makes me really happy is seeing somebody just, you know, be able to do it. Unfortunately, it's still rare enough that you can sort of look at somebody who's able to follow her heart, make a living out of it, have good solid personal relationships that are nourishing, and nod. And I wish it were not such a struggle. I wish it were still easier to be able to think about having a rewarding personal life—having children, having a career, and not having that be just a big, huge, impossible struggle.

Anthropological Commitments

Regardless of the particular career trajectory, these anthropologists, like the vast majority of our colleagues, are deeply committed individuals and professionals. While there are major shifts and great variation in what anthropologists devote their thinking and work to, we tend to be united in a commitment to the relevance of an anthropological perspective for critical engagement with some aspect of the world that needs analytic scrutiny. Likewise, we have seen through the examples offered in this chapter the way that anthropologists across subfields, areas of study, and work locations are quick to focus on the utility of anthropological perspectives for enduring human issues and the importance of finding ways to disseminate our work to the public. Some have been effective and others much less so. How to do so effectively often remains elusive. Although some anthropologists find it possible, others do not necessarily see clear opportunities, audiences, or ways forward.

We think some things are changing, and they matter to anthropologists like Monica Heller, Carolyn Sargent, and Jacqueline Comito. But sadly, we think that there will probably always be challenges for people who care about social justice, equality, and all of humanity, and this means that anthropologists of all sorts will continue to have passions—obsessions, as some of us would call them—and frustrations elicited by the inequalities that continue to exist around them. We think that there will long be room for anthropologists to contribute to humanity, acknowledging their own failings, their professional pasts, and their own areas of expertise. Critique is important to us all, and we are convinced that it will continue to be that way for generations to come as a fundamental aspect of flawed and ever-changing human societies.

6

Thinking like and with Anthropologists

●●●●●●●●●●●●●●●●●●●●●●●●

As we talked with and listened to our colleagues, they often shared narratives from their anthropological lives that were outside the scope of our planned inquiries about personal and professional origins, trajectories, and experiences. Like most forms of conversational exchange, our discussions spawned creative moments of spontaneity when we learned a good deal more about anthropological lives, passions, and perspectives than we anticipated. Following this inductive path of emergent understanding that is so central to disciplinary methods and analytic research in anthropology, we take up some of these diverse threads and bring them together in what we see as aspects of a distinct disciplinary way of knowing that anthropologists across the professions and subfields will recognize.

Some of these underlying analytic perspectives that anthropologists share can be productively understood as bringing to light and questioning taken-for-granted assumptions and ideas about the way the world works. Michael Herzfeld, somewhat cheekily, calls anthropology a gadfly discipline, meaning one that often agitates and provokes others by constantly questioning accepted truths. Theoretically oriented scholarship has called this epistemological position anthropology's interrogation and critique of "common sense" in particular, concrete, historical, and ethnographic contexts (Herzfeld 2001; Engelke 2018). These ethnographic contexts where local "common sense" logics are scrutinized range from a European genetics lab to coca farms in the Bolivian highlands. Moreover, the analyses they produce pay attention to the ways that both ordinary and authoritative explanations of how the world works are linked to hegemonic systems of inequality. In other words, anthropologists are trained and eager to notice the unnoticed, hear silences as meaningful, and turn accepted explanations upside down, studying them from the opposite perspective with an eye toward the systems they support.

The insights offered by this group of anthropologists raise wildly different topics that range from primate evolution to the Olympics. Taken together as a partial representation of anthropological thinking, the perspectives offered here show close attention to unconsidered forms of sameness, a deep concern with classification and regulation, a focus on implicit forms of inequality, and even the place of the metaphysical in secular anthropological work. As we have already said, anthropologists work on a wide variety of things related to humans, but analysis and critique loom large in all cases, and this chapter aims to show how those practices emerge organically through the habits of the mind and embodied experiences as an anthropologist.

Sameness

Many people associate anthropology with the study of cultural difference and diversity across time and space; this common perspective often becomes codified in higher education when anthropology courses count for general education requirements concerning diversity and cultural difference at colleges and universities. However, true to the disciplinary proclivity to question commonly accepted perspectives, including our own, we found the anthropologists we spoke with thinking about shared and collective sameness. As Virginia has explained and explored in her own research, sameness is presupposed and has an anteriority when conceptualizing notions of difference. In other words, sameness is just as much a product of collective thinking and effort as difference is. Moreover, people learn to think about certain things and certain people as the same and certain other things and other people as different throughout socialization across the lifespan. In this book, and in our engagement with twenty other anthropologists, we see individuals considering forms of sameness across species lines and the sameness of human generosity across domains and communities.

We begin with a longer excerpt from the conversation between Virginia and Agustín Fuentes, who said,

> And so I don't think anyone . . . [It] has to go beyond just thinking about humans or even particular things about humans. I think it is a valid anthropological question to extend the gaze a little bit past our own worlds to the worlds of related organisms like primates, but . . . I think the human-other interface is also one of the most important [and] exciting areas in anthropology.

There are [some types of sociality across species] long term. There are a couple of ways we can think about the interactions. There is conflict because of the shared space. There is a commensalism where they do just share space. There is competition over food and utilization of the shared space, but there are also social and physiological histories. I mean, if we look throughout much of Asia, we see very interesting social, religious, and traditional things that have this collaboration and attraction between humans and macaques. Bruce Wheately wrote a great study of this a number of years ago, and a number of people have looked at this, particularly with macaque monkeys and different Southeast Asian, East Asian, and South Asian cultures. There are those types of interactions. There are those Lisa Engell, George Engell, and their group [have] demonstrated, a substantial possibility for overlap of pathogens in a mutual exchange of viruses and diseases for centuries, if not millennia, and so I would argue that the similarity between humans and macaques and this overlap has also led to a mutual evolution where we influence one another.

Virginia replied by asking Agustín to elaborate, especially because she was worried that what he said could be misunderstood. She asked,

As you talk about it, I am thinking there has been a tendency in anthropology over many years (and, of course, there are exceptions) for many people to be interested in certain kinds of communities—and even when they recognize that obviously those people live in the world and have connections to others (whether it is a big political state or a big neighboring community), there has often been a desire to want to understand a group of people within a smaller setting. I think that also, maybe less so now than most of the twentieth century, it has led to the study of people that tends to highlight their supposed difference from others and downplay interactions.

Agustín responded,

Yes, I absolutely agree, and I can even argue that ethno-primatology sort of lags behind that transition in social anthropology for about a decade. People have been doing it a long time, but in the late eighties, I think, that became more common, and I think that today it would be hard to get away to study the "Ooga Booga" somewhere as a unique entity. I think the interesting part of reality is that it has become more accepted, of course, that there is this incredible layer and web of interconnectivity and it is that web (maybe) and the position of the people and their interests within that web and their interconnections that is of interest. And you're right, political economists have been doing this for a while, as have political ecologists, but I think it is becoming a more dominant trend. I think it is by necessity. I don't think you can ignore those kinds of connections. But those are the connections that I always found most interesting. It is the idea that comes from evolutionary training in one sense and a good training in ethnography. It is the idea that culture, like organic units, is not static and has never been static, that evolution is ongoing, as is cultural [formation], however you define it. The bottom line is that things don't stay the same. There are trends, similarities, and homologies and things that pass from generation to generation, but there is this constant dynamic flux. So there has always been that dynamism that interests me—maybe more so than the static snapshot that was the classical anthropological representation that I think is no longer a dominant trope.

Virginia asked,

You're not worried that in the process of focusing too much on interconnectivity and multiple species, the anthropos in anthropology (with its emphasis on the human) will sort of disappear and then we will somehow become like an ancient and long-gone community of thinkers and scholars?

Agustín replied,

No, I think there is never going to be a shortage of people wanting to look at the very minute details of just being a human or just one minor aspect of being human. I have no doubts about that. I think our contemplation of us as alone in the universe or even in our own bodies is no longer with us. The whole microbiome studies—I mean there are more and more, and if you add up all the genes of the organisms who live on our bodies, they outnumber us by millions to one. I think it is an artificial representation to think of us standing alone in some unique position in the universe.

Agustin thinks big. He thinks about humans but always in relation to living nonhumans. It is not necessarily the way all anthropologists think and work today, but he is far from alone in these thoughts.

Listen, for example, to Tom Boellstorff talking with Virginia about the kind of affective social relations that often characterize anthropologists' professional interactions in the field and among peers.

Virginia observed,

Maybe we're wiser and we're actually spotting kindness where earlier in our lives we might have mostly been consumed by the wrongs that we wanted righted.

Tom agreed, stating,

I think it's been kindness all the way around and, you know, maybe that's because I'm a Pollyanna or maybe because I've been fortunate but, you know, even with Indonesia or whatever, there's obviously heterosexism and homophobia and injustice and meanness in that sense, but gay and lesbian and transgender Indonesians have been so incredibly kind to me—taken me in, given me so much time and attention, and taken care of me, and I could still never repay everything that they have done. I'll never be able to, and that kind of kindness that people have given me in that sense has just been unending. It has just blown me away how incredibly kind people have been.

And then in virtual worlds or online games, in some virtual games like *World of Warcraft*, which is a virtual world but very game oriented, there's even verbs like *twinking*—like a twinkie, twinking—where people will give you something for free, and this happens in *Second Life* all the time as well. It's amazing how much kindness there is. I think people often assume because of anonymity that people will be mean and, if you look at the comments on CNN .com or something, you see people saying all kinds of mean stuff, but anonymity can also lead to incredible kindness. And also in virtual worlds, it's not always anonymous because you get to know people, and even if you only know their screen name, that's a real identity that you get to know and then it's not really anonymous anymore and there's incredible kindness. People in *Second Life* who run entire educational institutions—schools—that are for helping people who are new—to show them how to do stuff—where they teach classes every week, all for free. I mean, it's just incredible [to see] the amount of kindness that people will do for each other in those spaces.

And then, you're absolutely right [about kindness] in the world of editing, too. That was a big shock for me as well now. You know, having done this for four years, I say in all of my editors' letters that here are the editors' and the reviewers' comments and then I put in parentheses "redacted"—that I redact the comments from the reviewers. If there's something inappropriate, they don't need to see that. I take that out. And what's been shocking to me is that in four years, I've probably had to redact like that maybe two or three times. I mean, less than once a year. It is shocking how nice people are. I have almost never had to redact, but it has been shocking to me how really generous people are with their comments. Even if they think that it should be rejected, [they] still take the time to offer ideas to revise it, to submit it to another journal. I've just been taken aback, really, by how kind people are.

These reflections encourage us to recognize patterns of generosity in our professional experiences as anthropologists. We may associate analysis and critique with negativity and criticism but, as Tom has stated, anthropologists often find the opposite; in fact, a good deal of the very endeavor of anthropology as a field of practice relies fundamentally upon the generosity of others who allow anthropologists into their lives in some professional capacity. Finding patterns of any kind is a way of asserting sameness, as well as difference.

Notice how this shows up in Sarah Francesca Green's observations:

> If you have difference, then there must also be a concept of sameness. And that's something that in anthropology we haven't maybe paid as much attention to. . . . In a way, that also comes from my background, because I was sort of thinking, well, if I am English, having grown up in Greece, what makes me the same as other English people, and not the same as other Greek people?

In all these instances, we highlight that sameness is perceived and cultivated each time social difference is invoked, and those processes are central to anthropological investigation across subfields, geographies, and temporalities. Sarah grew up being told by her parents that she was English, even though she spent most of her childhood in Greece. In some ways, this was a mystery to her, but it may also have led her to become an anthropologist when she grew up. As she puts it, "What makes me the same as other English people, and not the same as other Greek people?" Her question, like those of all the anthropologists represented in this book, can be a matter of empirical investigation.

Implicit Forms of Inequality

Anthropologists have also long been concerned both ethically and intellectually with various kinds of exclusion and the inequalities that they often justify and naturalize. Among many anthropologists, we find close attention to persistent forms of inequality that deal with everyday forms of exclusion that often go unnoticed in multilingual, multiethnic, and multiracial contexts. This kind of close attention is conditioned by years of disciplinary thinking; it becomes habitual. It would be a mistake to think that it just reflects individual preferences in some abstract way. Some of the colleagues interviewed and quoted here were especially clear about that, but it is a very long-standing concern for many, and perhaps most, anthropologists.

Consider Monica Heller's reaction to the Olympics in Vancouver. She was not working on the Olympics or anything related to sports at the time. She just reacted to what she saw and heard, and we think it is a good example of how thinking like an anthropologist extends far beyond one's formal research. When Virginia mentioned the Olympics in Vancouver, Monica said,

> So that's Canada. And a lot of us are very angry because it was a very Anglo presentation. So there's a lot of very, very angry people out there because of what was felt as just a kind of, "Oh whoops, we forgot about the francophones

again." But the point that makes me angry is that it's partly this kind of blithe, um, "Oh whoops, forgot about you," and not—and it happens to be about francophones. It happens to be in my face right now because of the opening ceremonies, and there's all kinds of stuff going on in the past and so on, but it's that kind of innocent domination.

"Oh, oh, so what do you think is the big deal about?" You know, whether it's gender politics or it's race politics, it doesn't matter. But that kind of, "Well, we can't do it—it would cost too much," or, you know, I've got a list of all of the excuses that I've heard all over the world and they're all the same. It really doesn't matter who's involved, but they're [similar]—"We forgot," "We didn't think about it," "We've never done it before," "It costs too much." There's probably two or three others that I can't remember off the top of my head but that are always the same, and it's always that you end up being the crazy one for complaining. . . . It's the lack of attention that comes out of not having to think about the Other.

I mean there was a lot of attention paid to First Nations, which was completely appropriate and needed to be done. It was good, and I haven't spoken to representatives of the Inuit or First Nations, but there was some discontent there. There were some comments about folklorization and some issues about the totem pole and the bear, which was supposed to be the spirit bear, and some people said it looked like the polar bear in the Coca-Cola commercial. So there are some issues there.

But with the French stuff—for example, [in the Olympics] there were segments about different parts of the country, and each one of them was introduced with a quote from a writer or a famous person of some kind. One of the first ones was a quote from a French Canadian poet, François-Xavier Garneau, which was translated into English and read by Donald Sutherland, who can speak French perfectly fine, as far as I know. There was no reason why it had to be translated into English except that somebody thought it had to be translated into English. Or it could have been translated into x—everything could have been translated into both, but there was just, "We're not going to." So there was nothing; none of those quotes were actually done in French. . . . So there was one song in French sung by a francophone right at the very end. None of the others were. In the representation of the country, we had the North and the snow and the *aurore boréale*—the northern lights—and the Rockies, the Pacific Ocean, and the prairies. And then [in representing] the whole kind of center East, [there] were these maple leaves and fiddlers, which is both an Anglo-Eastern and a francophone tradition, but there was nothing that showed you that there was anything francophone about it, although that was an available thing to signal in some way. So I think it would have been very easy to do, but they just didn't.

Clearly Monica was quite passionate about this, and we could easily have put this excerpt in the chapter on passions, but we also wanted to illustrate what it means to think like an anthropologist, even when someone is not in the midst of research on a specific topic. So Monica's thoughts about the Olympics in Vancouver seemed more fitting here, because they demonstrate a critical anthropological perspective applied more generally to the life that unfolds around us organically.

Lee D. Baker also talked quite a bit about explicit and implicit forms of inequality. We include only the parts of that conversation that seem especially representative of anthropological thinking. He started with his experience teaching at Duke but quickly moved on to relationships between racialized homogeneity and admissions and academic administration in higher education:

> I have a large following of Asian American students in my classes, and I think it is because I have the sensitivity and understand, really understand, the diversity of the Asian American experience. And just maybe it is because of my growing up, I'm not sure. Where I do push this is at the very top administrative level. I mean we, . . . when we look at diversity, we lump Koreans, Japanese, and Chinese [together], whether they are international or U.S. together, and that does not do anything for the Hmong, the Vietnamese, the Cambodians, the Laotians, or the Filipinos. In terms of even admissions, understanding that is important (if we're committed to diversity). I keep pushing that we cannot just lump all Asian students together. We have to be more sensitive and nuanced and, if we are really committed to diversity, what do we do? We have to separate. We can't just say "Asian" and "Pacific Islander." We have to look and drill down and say, "Is this person a kid [or] a grandkid [of] a refugee or a recent immigrant?" That is the aspect of this that I think growing up on the West Coast, being part of that Pacific Rim, you know, you immediately understand [that] there is more diversity within the Asian American community. And it is not all equal.

Another striking example comes from an exchange between Virginia and Shannon Lee Dawdy when their conversation turned toward social stratification and the ways that it affected talk about, and efforts around, Hurricane Katrina in New Orleans.

Virginia stated,

> I sometimes thought that there were ways in which people in the greater New Orleans area talked about class that exceeded what I sometimes find in other parts of the country. Perhaps they talked indirectly about class, and maybe that is something that many of us in the country do, but in some ways in New

Orleans I thought it wasn't so much mentioning, "Well, I'm upper class," or so-and-so is lower-middle class.

Shannon responded,

No, no, no, it's like, What high school does she go to? And how we'll identify you by class as well as by color. . . . There are other ways in which definitely the response to Katrina, the national, international response to Katrina, was about this cultural treasure—this whole city that produced an incredible music tradition, incredible food tradition, was just a special place or that people had special memories of going to as tourists. [There is always] the exceptionalism. So I guess I'm saying it served whatever purpose people needed in terms of their public politics. . . . New Orleans is the tragedy that occurred. There was [a tendency to say that it was] highly typical of the racial inequalities and [that] this persists across particularly urban landscapes in the United States, or [that] it was highly atypical and is atypical and, therefore, needs dramatic rescue efforts, and you saw this in the way that musicians, in particular, received incredibly rapid and generous aid. I think that's a marvelous thing. But it's, if you look at the numbers and you look at infrastructurally what they received, it's far and it's out of whack, shall we say. Or let's put it this way: It identified musicians as a special case, and they received a disproportionate amount of assistance, far and above what a brick worker would have or a hotel worker would have received. It vaulted them into a privileged class. That's very interesting, but it's emblematic of the way New Orleans is held up as a special and exceptional culture—which it is, I'm not denying that. But I'm just saying [that] these major events can play into all kinds of politics.

Inequality is something most anthropologists care about deeply, and the colleagues we interviewed for this book echoed that. We are also trying to deepen that understanding here. Inequality does not just happen. It is based on conceptions of sameness and difference that prevail, and those have consequences. Anthropologists tend to track their impact on people, even when it is not part of their official job.

Regulation

Another theme that emerged when talking with our colleagues about their anthropological lives was social regulation. Many anthropologists focus on this in their work, and we heard that in the interviews we conducted for this book. Such work brings attention to ways that some bodies, identities, and images of others are surveilled, regimented, and disciplined by various people and institutions across a variety of disparate social contexts. At issue in forms of social regulation are enduring questions of value and belonging quite central to anthropological inquiries across areas of specialization throughout the history of the discipline. Right now in many countries—including the United States— we face border questions, questions about mobility and discrimination, refugee status, and unequal treatment of migrants. This is very current. There have been other issues in the past, and there will no doubt be other issues in the future. Sometimes these things are not spotted by others; sometimes they are. But they always matter to anthropologists. Notice the observations we quote here and the way anthropology has led to them.

Marilyn Strathern is a great example. She is well known for her work on gender, as well as on audit systems. And, as we have noted before, she has been a very influential figure in social anthropology in the United Kingdom for many years. Partway through her career, she chose to turn her anthropological thinking and research to the UK and continental Europe, and not just to Papua New Guinea, where she had started out as an anthropologist. In her conversation with Virginia, she talked more about that work than about her earlier work, on which she had established her academic career. Virginia probed into other aspects of her life and work, too, but Marilyn focused on more recent observations and thoughts, as well as her feelings about them. Here we focus on what she said about social and political regulation.

Marilyn told Virginia,

> I wrote an article about the fascinating way in which audit has its roots in systems of accounting, which, in turn, have their roots in a revision of the examination system that took place in eighteenth-century Europe and sort of rounded the circle. [I did this] by looking at the complaints of academics and what they think was simply a model coming from accounting and realizing that that model, in turn, came from the forms in their own system. And in the course of doing this, I actually footnoted (I think) about five places where I was borrowing from PNG [Papua New Guinea] ethnography in that situation. But, more interesting, I am at the moment doing some work for the Nuffield Council on Bioethics,[1] who've asked me to chair a working party to consider various factors in relation to organ, gamete, blood donation, body parts, and the works. Primarily, this is for the UK. . . . But, of course, in the back of my mind all the time is the way in which people I know in islands of Papua New Guinea think about those sorts of things and think about compensation, remuneration, and all the rest of it. And it sharpens my appreciation of the cultural particularities of the UK. . . .

[1] The Nuffield Council on Bioethics is a British council dedicated to questions of bioethics, and it is interesting but also promising that a senior anthropologist like Marilyn Strathern should be involved.

I don't think I'd appreciated it until recently. Some of the literature that we're having to look at [leads me to think this way]—the extent to which bodies are significant to persons in the context we live in and the tenacity with which people think of, or are attached to, or think about bodies, body parts.... The issue that lies behind the Nuffield Council's request is the increasing [issue of regulation]. We're talking about regulated societies, of course, not unregulated trade. We're talking about the context of underregulation. The issue that the Nuffield Council asked me to [examine] is the perceived and continuing shortage of bodily material of all kinds for treatment and for research, and all kinds of questions, of course, about what a shortage is. That was the rationale.

Virginia asked,

And since much of this does involve a society that is clearly quite into regulation right now, do you sometimes (in doing this work, or having agreed to do this work) worry that you are extending, deepening, or participating in what you yourself have critiqued as audit culture?

Marilyn responded,

Very much so, but the participation is unavoidable, and always was unavoidable. And I think in relation to the audit culture—that was never a critique that intended to come from outside the system. It was an attempt to make sense of parts of the system that one is embedded in and committed to excesses.... I remember getting up before an undergraduate audience—I think it was at SOAS in London[2]—and complaining about the audit culture. But, of course, I was also administering as head, and a student got up and said, "Well, what are examinations then?" I mean, we're—we're part of a system. And I think, in fact, in the Nuffield Council situation, I have to work very hard to be part of the system rather than imagine I'm commenting from some sort of outside place.... There's a working party composed of extremely interesting and committed people, both directly concerned with some of these issues but, professionally speaking, and not concerned, I mean coming at it from a distance. They're an interesting working party, and I'm at a sort of stage of thinking along with people.

Marilyn is keen to think about structures that oblige people to participate in forms of regulation. Sarah Francesca Green, who was trained at Cambridge

[2] This is a reference to the London-based School of Oriental and African Studies. Its official name is SOAS, University of London. It is an institution that has long been focused on the study of Asia, Africa, and the Middle East.

University and worked with Marilyn there, mentioned regulation as well in her conversation with Virginia, but she brought it up in a very different context. As we have said before, Sarah has a personal background that is quite different from Marilyn's, and in the following excerpt she brought those individual experiences up, along with matters of social and political regulation that manifested in regular forms of everyday discourse.

Sarah recollected,

I was constantly being told by my [English] parents and by others that I wasn't actually a Greek and that I was English and that, therefore, the place where I came from was England, and . . . I remember looking at a map that my mother had sent from England. We did some home schooling sometimes when I was young, and I would sit and stare at it for long periods of time because I was trying to compute exactly what England was because I didn't really travel when I was young. . . . I never went to England, never went to any other country, actually, the whole ten years I was in Greece.

Virginia probed,

But who was telling you that you were English? Just your family? Your parents?

Sarah explained,

No, everybody we knew. We were, you know, οι ξένοι (e xenoi), "the foreigners." It wasn't seen as a derogatory term. I mean, *foreign* sounds much more derogatory [in English] than it does in Greek, ξένοι (xenoi). . . . And my parents, you see, didn't speak [contemporary Greek] well. My father speaks very good Greek, but he tends to pepper it a little bit with classical Greek.

I think the other very big issues that made me not Greek were a gender issue and religion. We never went to the Orthodox church and everybody else did, and that was a big issue. The gender part, that was a very big part of it, you know. There was a very big difference in what girls and boys could do in those days, and girls could not go out walking and running and jumping up and down and climbing trees and so on at will, and I did. My parents allowed it and encouraged it, maybe.

A third thing was actually animals. Greece has changed a very great deal, but in those days, there were a lot of kind of stray cats and dogs and things and the three of us—me and my two brothers—would gather them up quite often and bring them into the house. So the house was overrun with various kinds of pets, and that was completely out of the question [in most Greek households at the time], to bring [animals] into your house in those days. Cats and dogs. There were cats and dogs that were associated with lots of neighboring houses, but they never went in, ever, ever, ever. That was a very big distinction between inside and outside.

One of the things that happened when we moved from Mytilene to Athens was that I got quite a lot of flack from the Athenians about what was called Nishiotika, which is island-hick-accent Greek. I had to learn very, very rapidly the bourgeois Athenian accent because I just really didn't like being made fun of.

So that was an interesting experience and then, of course, listening to my parents, and I suppose I'm speaking mostly with my kind of parental accent now, which has been slightly altered, again because my parents speak what's known as the Queen's English. It's a very what we call "cut-glass" accent. They [my parents] sound like me except even more cut glass. I had to, as it were, lower the tone a bit because actually it's quite difficult to live in Manchester with a totally cut-glass accent. It's class issues. One of the things that gets very rarely talked about in England is that the further north you go, the class composition changes.

In both Greece and England, people notice accents quite a bit and place individuals in regions and socioeconomic classes based on them. This happens in some other countries, too, but often other forms of social classification loom larger. The United States is a good example. Some accents sound more cultured than others, but region and race often loom larger.

Other forms of regulation came up when Virginia talked with João Biehl, even when the topic veered to photography and his work with Torben Eskerod, his friend and collaborator. Virginia asked him whether he worried about photography freezing people up, making them seem like objects set in a time and place. She added that Eskerod's photographs are stunning but that she could also imagine people wondering why he, João, included them in his book *Vita*. To this João replied,

Sometimes we overburden the visual representer or the photographer and the artist in order to give the full context [of something], and that's asking too much, but that is honest and simple. [The photographer is] truthful to himself. It is representation, but based on what he saw. And the work of the larger context and the connections and of the world—in this it was for me to do this work, to restore context to those lives, and that means also to bring in dynamism. [So yes, it means] freezing to raise the question of temporality. So, you know, that is how I found peace with the question of representation. And I also think when I was doing this work, of course, in the nineties, the midnineties, the dominant work of critique of photography or representation was still one of, "Oh, you're commodifying people's suffering. How can you do that? People are not reducible to that." If one looks back, the person who set the tone for that type of critique was [Susan] Sontag in her work *On Photography* in the late seventies or early eighties, and she herself in her last book, *Regarding the Pain of Others*, said that she was wrong. She said that not to represent is equally a failure.[3] So maybe my expectation has been lowered from one that can actually demand [something] from someone who tries to represent.

Here the question of regulation is more implicit. It has to do with learned observations and critiques, and how someone consciously, much like Sarah, pays attention to it and responds to it. We include Sarah and João here because we do not find anthropologists always thinking explicitly about political and bureaucratic patterns, although many do. Anthropologists also notice ways people talk, ways people reproduce patterns they have learned, and ways that certain things become second nature to most people in a way that is often understood as "common sense." Noticing those patterns, reacting to them, and choosing ways to respond to them habitually are elements of what makes people anthropologists.

The Metaphysical and Analytical

In this section we and our colleagues take on binaries, their importance to people, and the ways that many anthropologists counter them in their work and their lives. Anthropology, in all of its diversity, is largely a product of the Enlightenment, after all, which is to say that its foundational assumptions are a product of eighteenth-century northern European society and culture. Thousands of anthropologists now exist and work outside northern Europe— indeed, outside the North Atlantic—and they tend to focus on issues that matter a great deal in their societies, but the entire field conceptually comes out of that particular historical and cultural moment of the European Enlightenment, so how to respond to those situated origins is a big and ongoing issue for many anthropologists around the world.

Social scientific thinking, as a product of that Enlightenment, drew on a division between the physical world and the metaphysical one, a binary distinction that also mapped onto secular and religious ways of knowing. Thus, as we have repeatedly shown in this book, anthropological lives are firmly grounded in a material world that is understandable through empirical investigation, something many of us just call fieldwork but that is often at times referred to

[3] Susan Sontag (1933–2004) was a very influential U.S. philosopher, many of whose works were read and discussed in a wide variety of communities. It is not surprising that João would mention her and two of her leading works, *On Photography* (1977) and *Regarding the Pain of Others* (2003). *On Photography* comprises a series of essays published between 1973 and 1977 in the *New York Review of Books*.

as participant observation, along with the collection of interviews, narratives, and quantitative data. Yet, as professionals in a gadfly discipline (drawing again on Herzfeld's phrase), anthropologists commonly work to question absolute notions of binary divisions in human life. Male-female, nature-nurture, humanities–social sciences, and good-evil are all conceptual divisions that anthropologists have challenged and disrupted in scholarly and public understanding to draw out more complexity and nuance in our understanding of humanity. Of course, there are more, but we focus on these because they have mattered a good deal to many of our colleagues, their lives, and their work. So, in this spirit, it is perhaps fitting that we conclude this chapter by turning to metaphysical and religious aspects of anthropological lives that were mentioned by a few of our colleagues.

Jacqueline Comito is a good example. She made her own belief system explicit in her reflections and her conversation with Brigittine, while Virginia raised the question of anthropological worldviews, the influence of religious ones, and notions of hope in her conversation with João.

Jacqueline stated,

> This is something that's a big no-no, that is, something not to talk about when we do academic work or if we're anthropologists: I'm also a practicing Catholic. And that frames a lot of who I am and how I deal with people. And I try to do right by people and some of it is just because . . . I'm a good enough anthropologist to understand some of the trappings of Christianity, and that's not the important part of it to me. The important part is an essence of being that was in the gospels. All the rest of that stuff is what has been created around it. So, you know, I could call myself a gospel Christian or Catholic. Then I am a gospel Catholic, you know. Do right by people.

Brigittine asked,

> Can we call you a Zen Catholic?

Jacqueline responded,

> Yeah, sure, I'm a Zen Catholic, because I like to self-teach and, after my mother died, I did a crash course in Zen Buddhism. I actually did. I went on a spiritual journey. That's a hard thing to do when you're in academia because it is so judged and so belittled.

Echoing Jacqueline's words about religiosity in the academy, Virginia pushed João hard, too. When he talked about Christianity and anthropology, she worried. Given his background in Christian theology, she asked him about hope and whether he thought that people reading him or hearing him as hopeful mattered to him. She also mentioned the fact that there are people (anthropologists, as well as others) perhaps not raised within the Christian world "who might hear you and somehow see you or think that yours is a deeply Christianity-grounded type of anthropology." Virginia then asked him,

> Has that ever come up? The idea of the soul or the individual? You never said the word *salvation*, but I can just imagine people in various parts of the world having something like this. Does this come up at all? Has anyone ever accused you of this? Not that I am accusing you.

João responded,

Of caring? No.

Virginia replied,

Oh, caring, that's true, of course.

João stated,

I hear you.

Virginia then clarified her question:

No, of Christianity.

João responded,

> A Christian thing? I think cynics could read this as an attempt to position oneself as a savior figure. We try to never endorse any other position that I take. [I am interested in any position] that helps people sustain a sense of anticipation. And I think it is something, I think it's much more analytic than religious. But I love the work of the economist Albert Hirschman.[4] He is the

---

[4] Albert Hirschman (1915–2012) wrote *A Bias for Hope: Essays on Development and Latin America* in 1971. Much of his published work in his later years was about hope, explicitly for Latin America. It is worth mentioning some of these other works here, since they have mattered a good deal to João. They include *The Passions and the Interests: Political Arguments for Capitalism before Its Triumph* (1977); *Essays in Trespassing: Economics to Politics and Beyond* (1981); *Getting Ahead Collectively: Grassroots Experiences in Latin America* (1984; with photographs by Mitchell Denburg); *The Rhetoric of Reaction: Perversity, Futility, Jeopardy* (1991); and *A Propensity to Self-Subversion* (1995).

social scientist of the possible. And he has a wonderful work called *A Bias for Hope*. And in the work that he did in the 1950s and sixties in Latin America following the Marshall Plan, the whole point was to deconstruct the idea that interventions and their models know what is right and what needs to be done. He said that people have capacities. People have ideas of the possible and people already have ideas of developing solutions themselves. I am very drawn to that. I like to call it the arts of existence. And in some ways that does not mean that people are not necessarily good in the end or that they will resolve everything into something positive. Often, it becomes deadly as well, so I am aware of that. There is a hope that interests me; indeed there is hope that fascinates me. The social lives of individual lives, of institutional lives, fascinate me.

Overall, the insights offered by this group of anthropologists went beyond the bounds of our focus on the profession of anthropology and its diverse career trajectories; nevertheless, they are central to understanding the professional lives made possible by engaging a disciplinary way of thinking. They point to the spaciousness of the discipline for innovative thinking, something most anthropologists find extremely appealing regardless of their institutional location.

We may not all agree with these anthropologists. Indeed, many anthropologists are agnostic or atheist, but not all. For most anthropologists, the issue that is not controversial is the desire to understand humanity in all its manifestations. There is also anger at discrimination and inequalities that may be explicit or implicit but that still privilege some people over others, and some societies over others. Beliefs vary, and anthropologists' interests vary, but this central aspect of being and living a life after becoming an anthropologist is a constant.

7

Conclusion

● ●

Anthropological
Lives Unbound

Anthropologists live lives that are varied, but they are also lives that reflect their choice to become professional anthropologists. In this book we have tried to show what these interesting and unique anthropologists are like, how they first encountered anthropology, why they chose to become professional anthropologists, what they do as anthropologists, what their passions are, and how those passions shape the work they do as anthropologists and the way they live their lives. We do so to give readers a sense of the range of possibilities available to those who choose anthropology as a career, as manifested in the diverse paths these anthropologists have chosen. Certainly there are other paths as well; but we hope that these possibilities will lead to discussion through consideration of the experiences and perspectives we have presented here.

We include our own experiences here, but we especially draw on the interviews and conversations we have had with twenty other anthropologists about their lives, their work, their passions, and the challenges they feel they face. These anthropologists have had a wide range of experiences both growing up and working as adults. Included here are the stories of colleagues born or raised in Argentina, Canada, England, Greece, India, and the urban and rural United States, not to mention an overview of Virginia's experience spending her early childhood in Cuba; her teens in Uruguay, Mexico, and Lebanon; and some of the times in between in New York, New Haven (Connecticut),

San Juan (Puerto Rico), and Fair Lawn (New Jersey). Featured also are anthropologists who identify themselves as primatologists, biological anthropologists, anthropological archaeologists, museum anthropologists, linguistic anthropologists, folklorists, applied or practicing anthropologists, medical anthropologists, social anthropologists, historical anthropologists, and cultural anthropologists. They are all united in being anthropologists, even though their specializations may be different.

Some of our colleagues first encountered anthropology in their childhood or adolescence, but the majority did not. Most of us first encountered anthropology when we took a course for our bachelor's degree. For most of us, finding anthropology was an eye-opening experience, and our lives were changed by that first encounter. We have tried to show here what we and our colleagues saw in anthropology that led us to eventually choose anthropology as a profession. For some people it was a specific topic—such as human evolution or linguistic diversity—but for many it was the approach, the commitment to a social understanding of the context of human life, or the way it illuminated something they were passionate about in new and exciting ways. In the choices people make, anthropology comes across as a particular framework for seeing and asking. It has inspired us, and it has drawn its past and current practitioners. The anthropological way of meeting the human world draws on a deep skepticism about unitary explanations that many people treat as common sense but that we find need analysis and exploration. The choice to become an anthropologist also implies a dedication to empirical evidence that generates more complicated and nuanced understandings of the world.

Featured here are people who have been fascinated with reproduction, human evolution, sexuality, gender, labor, agriculture, language, history, health care, notions of race in the United States and elsewhere, nationality, museum collections and exhibits, Native American life, inequality, ways to challenge existing power dynamics, government regulations, audit cultures, virtual realities, state violence, folk festivals, and claims to tradition. And these are just examples of the variety of topics, passions, and concerns we find when looking at the lives and works of any group of anthropologists. Others have had a passion for religion, households, sports, tourism, material remains, forensic work, failures, denials, and popular culture. We do not want to limit our discussion of anthropologists' passions to the passions the people we talked to have. They are just examples of the range of work anthropologists do. These perspectives are meant to invite others, whose voices are not represented here, into the discussion with their students, families, friends, and those curious to learn what is compelling about anthropology as a career choice and as a way of life.

We have also chosen to include the stories of people who have had a range of jobs in their lives after training as anthropologists to earn the terminal degree of PhD. Many have administered programs (some inside the academy and some outside it), several have been editors of scholarly journals or newsletters, many have supervised the research of others, and many have taught courses and advised students. Some have established awards, competitions, and innovative programs. Many have imagined, organized, and run scholarly conferences. Some reach out to the wider public through personal contacts, outreach programs, blogs, museum exhibits, and television appearances.

Many have learned and used a second, third, and even fourth language in their research, their teaching, their writing, and their advocacy. For some, this learning of other languages is taken for granted as just the way anthropologists do their work because of long-standing disciplinary understandings that there is vast diversity in how communities of people understand their world and that those perceptions are shaped by the languages we use in them. For others, it has been both a struggle and a commitment. It is a commitment because we deem it ethical under the circumstances. It is ethical because we acknowledge our privileged positions as native speakers of certain languages (English among them) and not the many others that people use in the world. In doing so, we also acknowledge our privileged positions as highly educated, and often class-privileged, members of our societies who have had the opportunity to study successfully at the graduate level. Anthropologists of all sorts want the world to be a more just place, and yes, many people who are not anthropologists share that hope and goal, but anthropologists typically make a point of having their work contribute to the effort to make the world a better place for all and not just for those who are already privileged. When anthropologists get mad, it is usually about inequality and discrimination in the world in general, or specifically in the society or societies in which they live, work, or do both. Some of the time their research, teaching, writing, and advocacy focus on Indigenous people and the way they have been conquered, subjugated, and marginalized in so many of the societies in the world. Some of the time that work focuses on groups of people other than Indigenous people who have also been conquered, subjugated, and marginalized through slavery, forced labor, silencing, colonialism, unequal terms of trade, and representations. But some of the time it focuses on the middle classes, the urban and self-labeled urbane, and even on the most privileged holders of economic, social, or political power.

All anthropologists have to be willing to step outside their comfort zones while in the field in order to engage in professional life. An openness to making the familiar unfamiliar and the unfamiliar more familiar is key. It is a conceptual move that undergirds the persistent curiosity of professional anthropologists, as well as their search for complex answers. At the same time, in her presidential address to the American Anthropological Association (AAA), Virginia has suggested that, as a professional group, anthropologists do have "comfort zones" that may inhibit the profession from more deeply realizing its limitations in current professional practices (Dominguez 2012). In particular, she points to continuing professional issues with race and racism within anthropology, our awareness and lack of awareness of disability and how it affects our own colleagues, and ways in which we may act as participants in U.S. hegemony, often without even noticing that we do so (2012, 399–401).

Anthropologists study it all, teach it all, write it all, and approach it all. And anthropologists do all of these things as a group. When people in other fields think that anthropologists are just particularists—that is, that they just learn a language spoken by a few, study social life in small communities (past or present), and advocate for small-scale societies—they are both right and wrong. Many anthropologists do so out of respect for all of human diversity—biological, linguistic, historical, social, economic, and cultural. But as a profession, anthropology takes it all in, viewing humanity and its primate relatives in all their diversity. And they take this holistic view not just from the perspective of those now in power (or in power at particular moments in human history).

The anthropologists we draw on here have years of experience living in, trying to understand, and writing about places and people around the planet—in Indonesia and other parts of Southeast Asia, India, Israel, Papua New Guinea, Canada, the United States, the United Kingdom, Ireland, Catalonia (and the rest of Spain), Sardinia (as part of Italy and as an entity unto itself), Russia, Poland, Argentina, Bolivia, Brazil, Guatemala, and various other parts of Central America. Additionally, many other anthropologists also specialize in social life (past and present) in Mexico, Peru, Ecuador, Chile, Mali, South Africa, France, Malawi, Kenya, Uganda, Nigeria, Iran, Turkey, Pakistan, China, Japan, Australia, New Zealand, the Republic of Korea, and so many more.

World Anthropologies and Future Anthropologists

There is no country we can think of that has not been studied by anthropologists. It is probably also true these days that all countries have anthropologists in them, to judge by the ever-expanding membership of the World Council of Anthropological Associations, consisting of the heads of over fifty anthropological associations around the world. We also see this in the expanding interest and participation in the movement called World Anthropologies, which connects to, but also worries about, the anthropological communities in the North Atlantic, their historical influence on all of anthropology, and what counts as anthropology today around the world in terms of legitimacy and disciplinary authority. While the AAA has between ten thousand and twelve thousand members at any one time, there are thousands of anthropologists both in the United States and outside it who are not members of AAA but are clearly anthropologists by training and self-description. These include biological anthropologists, anthropological archaeologists, applied and practicing anthropologists, social and cultural anthropologists, linguistic anthropologists, medical anthropologists, and community college faculty in varying anthropological subdisciplines. What we have addressed here may reflect U.S. conditions of training and work more than those elsewhere, but we are convinced that the overall orientation, work, passions, and interests of anthropologists of all types and in all places are also echoed here in some way.

Some effort has been made in recent years to include anthropology in the secondary school curriculum of various countries. Interestingly, it is rarely taught at the secondary school level around the world, at least as anthropology. Some anthropological content may be included in history, biology, or social studies classes in high schools, but it is quite rare to find secondary schools anywhere offering courses in anthropology itself.

Many of our colleagues in the United Kingdom worked hard for some years to get college-prep courses[1] established there in anthropology, but the relevant government office shut it down after only a few years. Officials said that there were not many takers, that there were not many qualified teachers, and that they could not find enough qualified examiners. We do not think they gave it enough time or promoted it enough.

There is interest both in the United States and elsewhere in furthering anthropological education outside its usual university settings. For example, the AAA established a task force to explore this in 2011; the International Union of Anthropological and Ethnological Sciences has a Commission on Anthropology and Education; and it is a goal of the current leadership of the World Council of Anthropological Associations to bring anthropology (of all sorts) to the secondary schools of countries around the world. But many more people are going to have to understand the value of anthropology before the reach, usefulness, and work of anthropologists will be recognized and addressed at that level. We hope that this book is at least a step in that direction.

We are, of course, deeply interested in the future of anthropology and not just the contemporary nature of the field. We imagine future anthropologists sharing the basic attitudes and orientations we have detailed here, but also carving their own paths and pushing against and beyond our current categories and understandings. We imagine a continued concern with social justice, since we are too practical to imagine that the world will change quickly and that there will no longer be reason to advocate for greater social justice than we currently have. We hope that many anthropologists will continue to teach young people in colleges and universities, but we also hope that this teaching will extend to secondary schools, museums, and other venues in the public sphere that will

---

[1] The British secondary school system includes O levels and A levels. O levels are intended for youths up to the age of sixteen; A levels are more specialized and are typically completed in two years (at ages sixteen to eighteen and before entering university training).

be created by passionate and committed anthropologists. And we imagine that anthropologists in the future will use their learned skills to analyze, engage with, and even critique the societies they live in, the values they have been taught to cherish, and the conceptions of humanity that will surround them.

We also harbor the hope that much more of the world will see the value and usefulness of anthropology than is often the case now, and that we will see many more physicians, bankers, lawyers, diplomats, and schoolteachers in the future with a background in anthropology, as well as many more trained anthropologists engaging in policy development, ethical supervision, and community leadership. Some anthropologists already do this kind of work, as we have shown in this book, but we think it would be great if many more did; if many more people took anthropology in high school, college, or graduate school; and if many more people became anthropologists.

Predicting the future is not something we are accustomed to doing, but we have had some experience with it and will here hazard an educated guess that should hold for at least the next ten to twenty years. We expect many people encountering anthropology for the first time over the next decade or two—and using anthropology in their lives and work—to be passionate about the environment (particularly climate change and environmental justice); passionate about human rights (including historical and ongoing injustice for which the state bears responsibility); passionate about hunger, disease, and health care; passionate about capitalism and its alternatives; passionate about globalization and its claims; passionate about ethics (including the ethics of social research, the ethics of science, and the ethics of anthropology itself); passionate about ever-evolving technologies and their uses; and passionate about virtual realities and the social worlds they produce or reproduce. We believe they will also be passionate about violence, reproduction, and social change, particularly related to decolonization around the globe. These are, after all, broad enough to encompass matters of inequality, gender and sexuality, human exceptionalism, and our place on the planet. But there no doubt will also be other passions that arise, passions that engage future anthropologists, and passions that may only become obvious as the world changes. It is our hope that in the future there will be more anthropologists to continue to pursue the passions of a profession we have tried to explore here, and who will continue to face new challenges and to carry on the commitment and the caring that are the hallmarks of rich, diverse, and fulfilling anthropological lives.

Acknowledgments

The foundation of this book lies with Virginia Dominguez's deep dedication to the discipline and the profession of anthropology and her decades of tireless service to it, its practitioners, and its students. The foundation of our collaboration lies in what is now over twenty years of intensive, thoughtful, and inspiring conversations between the two of us about anthropology, its directions, its pasts, and its futures. We hope that this book provides a spark for many such exchanges among others who find something of value, something concerning, or something worth pursuing further in its pages.

We are very grateful to the twenty anthropologists who contributed to this book by allowing us to interview them, but we are also very grateful to Emily Metzner, Erin Benson, Amanda Butler, and Brenda Garcia, who helped produce this book by transcribing interviews and getting contributors' photos, bios, and selected readings. Virginia also wants to thank Damon Dozier, then staff member at the American Anthropological Association, who made it technologically possible for many of these interviews to be conducted by phone and recorded at AAA offices in northern Virginia. Sometimes there were glitches, but most of the time the system worked well, thanks to Damon. Virginia would also like to thank Bill Davis, then executive director of AAA, who allowed Damon to do this work.

It is impossible to count how many people helped us out when we chose to become anthropologists or when we worked to pass some of our passion on to our friends, family members, nonanthropologist coworkers, and neighbors. We should definitely thank our anthropological mentors and teachers. For Virginia, they include Susan Bean, Bernard Cohen, Harold Conklin, Henry Harpending, Ellen Messer, Sidney Mintz, Ralph Nicholas, Richard Price, Alison Richard, Ben (Irving) Rouse, Marshall Sahlins, Harold Scheffler, David Schneider, and Stanley Tambiah. For Brigittine, they include Florence Babb, Michael

141

Chibnik, Virginia Dominguez, Nora England, Laurie Graham, June Helm, and Margery Wolf.

We also want to thank those who have been colleagues at various institutions and have taught us in both formal and informal ways. For Virginia, these include Mahadev Apte, Matt Cartmill, Kathy (Katherine) Ewing, Richard Fox, Ernestine Friedl, Woody (Atwood) Gaines, William (Mac) O'Barr, Patricia Pessar, Naomi Quinn, Elwyn Simons, Carol Smith, Michel-Rolph Trouillot, Rob Weller, Brackette Williams, and Allen Zagarell at Duke; Steve Caton, Alison Galloway, Judith Habicht-Mauche, Susan Harding, Olga Najera-Ramirez, Loki (Triloki) Pandey, Richard Randolph, and Anna Tsing at the University of California, Santa Cruz; Michael Chibnik, Russell Ciochon, Nora England, Robert Franciscus, Laura Graham, Meena Khandelwal, Ellen Lewin, Douglas Midgett, Mac Marshall, Erica Prussing, and Margery Wolf at the University of Iowa; and Nancy Abelmann, Jessica Brinkworth, Matti Bunzl, Kate (Kathryn) Clancy, Jenny Davis, Brenda Farnell, Christopher Fennell, Susan Frankenberg, Alma Gottlieb, Jessica Greenberg, Faye Harrison, Cris Hughes, Petra Jelinek, Janet Dixon Keller, Lyle Konigsberg, Elise Kramer, Steve Leigh, Lisa Lucero, Alejandro Lugo, Kora (Korinta) Maldonado, Ripan Malhi, Martin Manalansan, Jeff Martin, Jayur Mehta, Ellen Moodie, Andrew Orta, Tim Pauketat, John Polk, Gilberto Rosas, Mahir Saul, Laura Shackelford, Helaine Silverman, Krystal Smalls, and Rebecca Stumpf at the University of Illinois at Urbana-Champaign.

Brigittine wants to thank her colleagues Meena Khandelwal at the University of Iowa and Jon Andelson, Vicki Bentley-Condit, Doug Caulkins, Xavier Escandell, Kathy Kamp, Jonathan Larson, Katya Gibel Mevorach, Kate Patch, Monty Roper, Maria Tapias, and John Whittaker at Grinnell College.

We want to thank the many students who have taught us over the years, even when we were technically teaching them. Virginia especially wants to thank Maddie (Madeleine) Adelman, Lauren Anaya, Scarlett Andes, Jamie Arjona, Magda Baligh, Becky Chan, Danielle Cunningham, Steve Edbril, Chibundo Egwuatu, Nadia Abu El-Haj, Ofira Fuchs, Isar Godreau, David Goldberg, Jenna Grant, Michele Hanks, Krista Harper, Tim Landry, Yvonne Lasalle, Katie Lee, Evelyn Legare, Judith McDade, Emily Metzner, Murli (Balmurli) Natrajan, Nina (Cristina) Ortiz, Nancy Press, Lavanya Murali Proctor, Mike Scher, Kenda Stewart, Andria Timmer, and Liza Youngling.

Brigittine wants to thank especially Maya Andelson, Hannah Boggess, Ryan Carlino, Payson Dai, Katie Fenster, Nathan Ford, Mona Ghadari, Elise Hadden, Joe Hiller, Mari Holmes, Patrick Kinley, Lauren Knapp, Misha Laurence, Emma Lawler, Nathan LeBlanc, Izzy Leo, Tiffany Matzas, Ayesha Mirzakhail, Scott Olson, Aric Pearson, Mary Powell, Emily Ricker, Heather Riggs, Zasha Russell, Grace Marengo Sanchez, Louisa Silverman, Sidonie Straughn-Morse, Claire Thompson, Lucia Tonachel, and Huaming Yu.

Claire Branigan is a special link between our collaboration and our ongoing passion for the discipline. We are confident that, as an undergraduate at Grinnell College and a current doctoral candidate in anthropology at the University of Illinois at Urbana-Champaign, Claire embodies the best of the profession thus far and will continue to imagine anthropological lives in new and inspiring ways.

Israeli and Palestinian anthropologists have also taught Virginia much over the years, especially Eileen Basker, Yoram Bilu, Nurit Bird-David, Limor Darash, Jackie Feldman, Khaled Furani, Harvey Goldberg, Yehuda Goodman, Jasmin Habib, Don Handelman, Nadeem Harkabi, Rhoda Kanaaneh, Tamar Katriel, Andre Levy, Fran Markowitz, Pnina Motzafi-Haller, Amalia Sa'ar, Moshe Shokeid, and Alex Weingrod.

Guatemalan scholars in and of the country have taught Brigittine a great deal about anthropology, its limits, and possibilities. Special thanks go to Nikte' María Juliana Sis Iboy, Lolmay García Matzar, Waykan Benito Pérez, Telma Can Pixabaj, Jennifer Reynolds, Victoria Sanford, and B'alam Mateo Toledo.

We have been fortunate to work with the wonderful leadership at Rutgers University Press. Thanks to Marlie Wasserman for believing in our project, to Kim Guinta for endorsing it, and Jasper Chang for his professional expertise and support. We also thank the anonymous reviewers, who certainly helped us expand the book in ways we hope they recognize and appreciate.

About the Anthropologists

LESLIE C. AIELLO is an evolutionary anthropologist with special interests in the evolution of human adaptation, as well as in broader issues of evolutionary theory, life history and the evolution of the brain, diet, language, and cognition. Her primary work has been on the relationship between energetics and the evolution of locomotion, diet, and brain growth and maintenance. In collaboration with Peter Wheeler, she developed the expensive tissue hypothesis, which posits an inverse relationship between brain size and gut size mediated through the adoption of a high-quality animal-based diet. This work also provided the basis for a series of papers focusing on the relationship between energetics, growth and development, and the evolution of cooperation in hominin evolution, as well as on the evolution of the biological basis for human speech. She also coauthored *An Introduction to Human Evolutionary Anatomy* (with M. C. Dean), which has become a classic reference book for paleoanthropology.

Leslie received her BA and MA in anthropology from the University of California, Los Angeles, and her PhD in human evolution and anatomy from the University of London.

In 2005, Leslie became president of the Wenner-Gren Foundation for Anthropological Research, a large, private foundation devoted solely to the support of international anthropological research. She spent the majority of her academic career (1976–2005) at University College London (UCL), where she was professor of biological anthropology from 1995. She was also head of the UCL Anthropology Department from 1996 to 2002 and head of the UCL Graduate School from 2002 to 2005. She served as the comanaging editor of the *Journal of Human Evolution* from 1993 to 1999 and has been active with the media in the public dissemination of science and particularly human evolution.

She is a fellow of the American Association for the Advancement of Science and of the German National Academy of Sciences Leopoldina, and she is a member of the American Philosophical Society. She is immediate past president of the American Association of Physical Anthropologists and has served as an officer for a number of other professional societies and as an adviser to a variety of international anthropological institutions and initiatives. She is professor emerita (biological anthropology) at UCL, was the 2006 Huxley Memorial Medalist and Lecturer, and received an Honorary Fellowship from UCL (2007) and an honorary doctorate from the Universidad de Alcalá, Spain (2016).

Selected Publications

Aiello, Leslie C., and M. Christopher Dean. 1990. *An Introduction to Human Evolutionary Anatomy.* London: Academic Press.

Aiello, Leslie C., and Jonathan C. K. Wells. 2002. "Energetics and the Evolution of the Genus Homo." *Annual Review of Anthropology* 31:323–338. Invited contribution.

Aiello, Leslie C. and Peter Wheeler. 1995. "The Expensive Tissue Hypothesis: The Brain and the Digestive System in Human Evolution." *Current Anthropology* 36:199–221. With commentaries and reply.

———. 2003. "Neanderthal Thermoregulation and the Glacial Climate." In *Neanderthals and Modern Humans in the European Landscape of the Last Glaciation: Archaeological Results of the Stage 3 Project*, edited by Tjeerd H. van Andel and William Davies, 147–166. McDonald Institute Monographs. Cambridge, England: McDonald Institute for Archaeological Research.

Antón, Susan C., Richard Potts, and Leslie C. Aiello. 2014. "Evolution of Early Homo: An Integrated Biological Perspective." *Science* 345 (6192). https://doi.org/10.1126/science.1236828.

LEE D. BAKER is professor of cultural anthropology, African and African American studies, and sociology, as well as dean of academic affairs and associate vice provost at Duke University.

Lee seeks to understand how countries whose overarching narrative is about equality, justice, and democracy can have such inequality. Much of his work has been centered on contextualizing these concepts in historical terms. He has aimed to historicize anthropological theories and critically analyze them, particularly with regard to race and African American studies.

Lee earned a bachelor of science in anthropology and a certificate in black studies from Portland State University in 1989. He obtained his PhD from Temple University, where his doctoral adviser was Thomas C. Patterson. Lee completed his thesis, "Anthropology and the Construction of Race, 1896–1954," in 1994.

Lee taught at Columbia University from 1997 to 2000. He has been a resident fellow at Harvard University's W.E.B. Du Bois Institute, the Smithsonian's

National Museum of American History, Johns Hopkins University's Institute for Global Studies, the University of Ghana–Legon, the American Philosophical Society, and the National Humanities Center. Although he focuses on the history of anthropology, he has published numerous articles on a wide range of subjects from sociolinguistics to race and democracy. Lee is also the recipient of the Richard K. Lublin Distinguished Teaching Award.

Selected Publications

Baker, Lee D. 1998. *From Savage to Negro: Anthropology and the Construction of Race, 1896–1954*. Berkeley: University of California Press.

———. 2001. "Profit, Power, and Privilege: The Racial Politics of Ancestry." *Souls: A Critical Journal of Black Politics, Culture and Society* 3(4): 66–72.

———, ed. 2003. *Life in America: Identity and Everyday Experience*. Malden: Blackwell.

———. 2009. "Racism, Risk, and the New Color of Dirty Jobs." In *The Insecure American: How We Got Here and What We Should Do about It*, edited by Hugh Gusterson and Catherine Besteman, 140–159. Berkeley: University of California Press.

———. 2010. *Anthropology and the Racial Politics of Culture*. Durham, NC: Duke University Press.

JOÃO BIEHL is Susan Dod Brown Professor of Anthropology and Woodrow Wilson School faculty associate at Princeton University. He is also codirector of Princeton's Global Health Program.

João's main research and teaching interests center on medical and political anthropology, the social studies of science and religion, global health, ethnography, and critical theory, with a regional focus on Latin America and Brazil. In his ethnographic projects, he has explored how science and technology move from the laboratory to health policy and popular discourse, and from professional medicine to domestic economies and the intimate realms of bodily experience, particularly in contexts of stark inequality.

In recent years, João has authored the award-winning books *Vita: Life in a Zone of Social Abandonment* and *Will to Live: AIDS Therapies and the Politics of Survival*. These major book projects charted the new geographies and politics of access and marginalization that have emerged in Brazil alongside pharmaceutical globalization, particularly around mental illness and HIV/AIDS. They also elaborated on the forms of mobilization and circuits of care through which poor patients and families struggle to make livable lives in precarious environments.

Before joining the Princeton faculty in 2001, João was a National Institute of Mental Health postdoctoral fellow at Harvard University (1998–2000). He earned a doctorate in anthropology from the University of California at

Berkeley (1999) and a doctorate in religion from the Graduate Theological Union (1996). He received a master's degree in philosophy and undergraduate degrees in theology and journalism from academic institutions in Brazil.

João is the coeditor of the book series Critical Global Health at Duke University Press. A Guggenheim Fellow, he was a member of the School of Social Science and the School of Historical Studies at the Institute for Advanced Study and the Ethel-Jane Westfeldt Bunting Scholar at the School for Advanced Research. He was also visiting professor at the École des hautes études en sciences sociales. João received Princeton's Presidential Distinguished Teaching Award in 2005 and Princeton's Graduate Mentoring Award in 2012.

João is currently writing *The Valley of Lamentation*, a historical ethnography of the Mucker war, a religious conflict that shattered immigrant communities in southern Brazil in the late nineteenth century. He is also working on a book titled *Unfinished: The Anthropology of Becoming* and finalizing ethnographic research on the judicialization of the right to health and the metamorphosis of politics in Brazil.

Selected Publications

Biehl, João. 2007. *Will to Live: AIDS Therapies and the Politics of Survival*. Princeton, NJ: Princeton University Press.

———. 2013. *Vita: Life in a Zone of Social Abandonment*. Updated with a new afterword and photo essay. Berkeley: University of California Press.

Biehl, João, Byron Good, and Arthur Kleinman, eds. 2007. *Subjectivity: Ethnographic Investigations*. Berkeley: University of California Press.

Biehl, João, and Adriana Petryna, eds. 2013. *When People Come First: Critical Studies in Global Health*. Princeton, NJ: Princeton University Press.

TOM BOELLSTORFF is professor of anthropology at the University of California, Irvine. His research interests have included the anthropology of sexuality, globalization, virtual worlds, Southeast Asian studies, HIV/AIDS, and linguistic anthropology.

Tom earned his PhD in anthropology at Stanford University in 2000. He joined the Department of Anthropology at the University of California, Irvine, in 2002, receiving tenure in 2006. He was editor in chief of *American Anthropologist*, the flagship journal of the American Anthropological Association (AAA), from 2007 to 2012. He has been cochair of the Association for Queer Anthropology and recipient of a fellowship from the American Council of Learned Societies. He is the winner of the Ruth Benedict Prize, given by the Society of Lesbian and Gay Anthropologists.

Raised in Nebraska, Tom moved to California to obtain bachelor's degrees in linguistics and music from Stanford University. He engaged in HIV/AIDS and LGBT activism in the United States, Indonesia, Malaysia, and Russia, at times with the International Gay and Lesbian Human Rights Commission and the Institute for Community Health Outreach, where he worked as regional coordinator before entering graduate school in anthropology.

In addition to several edited books and monographs, his work has been published in *American Anthropologist, American Ethnologist, Cultural Anthropology*, the *Annual Review of Anthropology*, the *Journal of Linguistic Anthropology*, the *Journal of Asian Studies; GLQ: A Journal of Lesbian and Gay Studies*, and *Ethnos*.

Selected Publications

Boellstorff, Tom. 2005. *The Gay Archipelago: Sexuality and Nation in Indonesia*. Princeton, NJ: Princeton University Press.

———. 2007. *A Coincidence of Desires: Anthropology, Queer Studies, Indonesia*. Durham, NC: Duke University Press.

———. 2008. *Coming of Age in Second Life: An Anthropologist Explores the Virtually Human*. Princeton, NJ: Princeton University Press.

Boellstorff, Tom, and Bill Maurer, eds. 2015. *Data, Now Bigger and Better!* Chicago: Prickly Paradigm.

Boellstorff, Tom, Bonne Nardi, Celia Pearce, and T. L. Taylor. 2012. *Ethnography and Virtual Worlds: A Handbook of Method*. Princeton, NJ: Princeton University Press.

Leap, William, and Tom Boellstorff, eds. 2004. *Speaking in Queer Tongues: Globalization and Gay Language*. Urbana: University of Illinois Press.

JACQUELINE COMITO, PhD, is an anthropologist actively involved in research, extension, and outreach activities in the areas of water, watershed-based community activities, and environmental attitudes. She has directed two highly successful outreach and education programs at Iowa State University: Water Rocks! (winner of 2016 Environmental Excellence Award for Education) and Iowa Learning Farms. Her creativity and vision have propelled these programs to become highly successful and in high demand across Iowa. In 2018, she cofounded the Conservation Learning Group, a collaborative team to advance training, outreach, and research across conservation land use and cropping systems to increase overall sustainability. Jacqueline interacts with a variety of stakeholders, including farmers, interested citizens, teachers, youths, environmental groups, and agency personnel. She is as an award-winning video writer, director, and producer, as well as a music lyricist, producer, and musician. Her numerous awards include the 2015 Environmental Law Institute's National Wetlands Award for Outreach and Education and a 2012 DuPont Pioneer Women of Innovation Award.

Selected Publications

Comito, Jacqueline, producer and host. *Conservation Chat*. http://conservationchat .libsyn.com.

Comito, Jacqueline, Brandy Case-Haub, and Mark Licht. 2018. "Rapid Needs

Assessment and Response Technique." *Journal of Extension* 56 (2). https://www.joe
.org/joe/2018april/tt1.php.
Comito, Jacqueline, Jon Wolseth, and Lois Wright Morton. 2013. "Stewards, Business-
men, and Heroes? Role Conflict and Contradiction among Row-Crop Farmers in
an Age of Environmental Uncertainty." *Human Organization* 72 (4): 283–292.
Water Rocks! 2014. "Incredible Wetlands." Video, 23:18, March 4, 2014. https://www
.youtube.com/watch?v=H9XZwfCBEE4.

SHANNON LEE DAWDY is associate professor of anthropology and of social sciences
at the University of Chicago whose fieldwork combines archaeological, archival, and ethnographic methods with a regional focus on the United States, the
Caribbean, and Mexico. The central thread running through her work concerns how landscapes and material objects mediate human relationships,
whether this means an examination of the historical ecologies of capitalism or
a focus on the emotional trajectories of those who lost their intimate object
worlds to Hurricane Katrina. Her first book, *Building the Devil's Empire*, offers
"rogue colonialism" to explain how French New Orleans, and many colonies
like it, functioned outside state controls, developing a political economy loosely
moored to metropolitan interests. Her new book, *Patina: A Profane Archaeology*, investigates nostalgic practices surrounding antiques, heirlooms, historic
houses, and ruins. It argues that these practices provide a means of critiquing
the capitalist present and of bonding people together through a type of kinship. Her current research focuses on rapidly changing death practices in the
United States, particularly around disposition and transformation of the body.
Collaborating with a filmmaker on the work, she also explores what happens
when we turn an archaeological lens on contemporary life, and the possibilities of an artistic approach to anthropological questions (see http://www
.mystarmydust.com). Shannon is a recent MacArthur Fellow and has received
funding for her fieldwork from the National Science Foundation and the
National Endowment for the Humanities. For publication access, see https://
chicago.academia.edu/ShannonLeeDawdy.

Selected Publications

Dawdy, Shannon Lee. 2008. *Building the Devil's Empire: French Colonial New
Orleans*. Chicago: University of Chicago Press.
———. 2011. "Why Pirates Are Back." *Annual Review of Law and Social Science*
7:361–385.
———. 2016. *Patina: A Profane Archaeology*. Chicago: University of Chicago Press.
Hartnett, Alexandra, and Shannon Lee Dawdy. 2013. "The Archaeology of Illegal and
Illicit Economies." *Annual Review of Anthropology* 43:37–51.

VIRGINIA R. DOMINGUEZ is the Edward William and Jane Marr Gutgsell Professor of Anthropology (and member of the Jewish studies, Middle Eastern

studies, and Caribbean studies faculties) at the University of Illinois at Urbana-Champaign. She is also cofounder and consulting director of the International Forum for U.S. Studies (established in 1995) and coeditor of its book series, Global Studies of the United States. A political and legal anthropologist, she was president of the AAA from 2009 to 2011, editor of *American Ethnologist* from 2002 to 2007, and president of the AAA's Society for Cultural Anthropology from 1999 to 2001. In 2013 she helped the World Council of Anthropological Associations establish the Brazil-based Antropólogos sem Fronteiras (Anthropologists without Borders). Author, coauthor, editor, and coeditor of multiple books, she is perhaps best known for her work on the Caribbean (especially in *The Caribbean and Its Implications for the United States* [1981], with Jorge Dominguez), her work on the United States (especially in *White by Definition: Social Classification in Creole Louisiana* [1986]), and her work on Israel (especially in *People as Subject, People as Object: Selfhood and Peoplehood in Contemporary Israel* [1989]). Her most recent books are the coedited *America Observed: On an International Anthropology of the United States* (2017) and *Global Perspectives on the United States* (2017). Before joining the University of Illinois faculty in 2007, she taught at Duke University, the Hebrew University of Jerusalem, the University of California at Santa Cruz, the University of Iowa, and Eötvös Loránd University in Budapest. She has also been directrice d'études at the École des Hautes Etudes en Sciences Sociales in Paris, a Simon Professor at the University of Manchester, a Mellon Fellow at the University of Cape Town, a Morgan Lecturer at the University of Rochester, a research fellow at the East-West Center in Honolulu, and a junior fellow at Harvard University.

Selected Publications

Dominguez, Virginia R. 2017. "The Erosion of Academic Tenure in the U.S. and Its Ties to Public Neoliberal Anti-Intellectualism." *ANUAC* 6 (1): 29–33. Special forum edited by Filippo Zerilli and Tracey Heatherington.

———. 2017. "On Chutzpah Countries and 'Shitty Little Countries.'" In *Small Countries: Structures and Sensibilities*, edited by Ulf Hannerz and Andre Gingrich, 141–158. Philadelphia: University of Pennsylvania Press.

———, ed. 2018. "Walls, Material and Rhetorical: Past, Present, and Future." Special issue, *Review of International American Studies* 11 (1).

Dominguez, Virginia R., and Jane C. Desmond, eds. 2017. *Global Perspectives on the United States: Pro-Americanism, Anti-Americanism, and the Discourses in Between.* Urbana: University of Illinois Press.

Dominguez, Virginia R., and Jasmin Habib, eds. 2017. *America Observed: On the International Anthropology of the United States.* New York: Berghahn Books.

T. J. FERGUSON is a managing member of Anthropological Research, a research company in Tucson, where he is also a professor in the School of Anthropology at the University of Arizona. His main teaching and research interests center on southwestern archaeology; ethnography; historic preservation; repatriation; architecture; and land use. He was educated at the University of Hawaii at Hilo (BA, 1973), the University of Arizona (MA in anthropology, 1976), and the University of New Mexico (MA in community and regional planning, 1986; PhD in anthropology, 1993). T. J. specializes in archaeological and ethnographic research needed for historic preservation, repatriation, and litigation of land and water rights. His clients include Indian tribes, governmental agencies, and museums.

Selected Publications

Colwell-Chanthaphonh, Chip, and T. J. Ferguson. 2006. "Memory Pieces and Footprints: Multivocality and the Meanings of Ancient Times and Ancestral Places among the Zuni and Hopi." *American Anthropologist* 108 (1): 148–162.

———. 2010. "Intersecting Magisteria: Bridging Archaeological Science and Traditional Knowledge." *Journal of Social Archaeology* 10 (3): 425–456.

Ferguson, T. J. 2009. "Improving the Quality of Archaeology in the United States through Consultation and Collaboration with Native Americans and Descendant Communities." In *Archaeology and Cultural Resource Management*, edited by Lynne Sebastian and William D. Lipe, 169–193. Santa Fe: School of Advanced Research Press.

Ferguson, T. J., G. Lennis Berlin, and Leigh J. Kuwanwisiwma. 2009. "Kukhepya: Searching for Hopi Trails." In *Landscapes of Movement: The Anthropology of Paths, Trails, and Roads*, edited by James E. Snead, Clark L. Erickson, and J. Andrew Darling, 20–41. Philadelphia: University of Pennsylvania Museum of Archaeology and Anthropology.

Ferguson, T. J., and C. Colwell-Chanthaphonh. 2006. *History Is in the Land: Multivocal Tribal Traditions in Arizona's San Pedro Valley*. Tucson: University of Arizona Press.

Mills, Barbara J., and T. J. Ferguson. 2008. "Animate Objects: Shell Trumpets and Ritual Networks in the Greater Southwest." *Journal of Archaeological Method and Theory* 15:338–361.

BRIGITTINE M. FRENCH is professor of anthropology and chair of the Peace and Conflict Studies Program at Grinnell College. She is a linguistic and political anthropologist whose diverse body of research focuses on theoretical and ethnographic approaches to narrative and testimonial discourse, violence, rights, and democratic institutions in postconflict nations. Her first book, *Maya Ethnolinguistic Identity: Violence, Cultural Rights, and Modernity in Highland Guatemala*, was published in 2010 and received numerous laudatory reviews. Her newest book, *Narratives of Conflict, Belonging, and the State: Discourse and Social Life in Post-War Ireland*, examines the persistence and transformation of conflict and forms of violence in the newly democratic postcolonial Irish state during the 1930s. Her research has also appeared in the *Journal of Human Rights*, *American Anthropologist*, *Language in Society*, and the *Annual Review* *of Anthropology*, among others. Brigittine's research has been generously supported by the U.S. Fulbright Program and the American Philosophical Society. She was a visiting scholar at the School of Applied Languages and Intercultural Studies at Dublin City University in 2012. She is deeply honored to have written this book with Virginia Dominguez and is deeply dedicated to her students at Grinnell.

Selected Publications

French, Brigittine M. 2009. "Technologies of Telling: Discourse, Transparency, and Erasure in Guatemalan Truth Commission Testimony." *Journal of Human Rights* 8 (1): 92–109.

———. 2010. *Maya Ethnolinguistic Identity: Violence, Cultural Rights, and Modernity in Highland Guatemala.* Tucson: University of Arizona Press.

———. 2012. "The Semiotics of Collective Memories." *Annual Review of Anthropology* 41:337–353.

———. 2018. *Narratives of Conflict, Belonging, and the State: Discourse and Social Life in Post-War Ireland.* New York: Routledge.

AGUSTÍN FUENTES is the Rev. Edmund P. Joyce, C.S.C., Endowed Chair in Anthropology at the University of Notre Dame. His research delves into the how and why of being human. From chasing monkeys in the jungles and cities of Asia, to exploring the lives of our evolutionary ancestors, to examining what people actually do across the globe, Agustín is interested in both the big questions and the small details of what makes humans and our closest relatives tick.

Agustín completed a BA in zoology and anthropology and an MA and PhD in anthropology at the University of California, Berkeley. He examines human evolution from several perspectives, and his research sheds light on some of the most common misconceptions about human nature, specifically in the areas of race, sex, and aggression. His current foci include cooperation and bonding in human evolution, ethnoprimatology and multispecies anthropology, evolutionary theory, and public perceptions of, and interdisciplinary approaches to, human nature(s).

Selected Publications

Fuentes, Agustín. 2008. *Evolution of Human Behavior.* Oxford: Oxford University Press.

———. 2010. "Naturalcultural Encounters in Bali: Monkeys, Temples, Tourists, and Ethnoprimatology." *Cultural Anthropology* 25 (4): 600–624.

———. 2010. "The New Biological Anthropology: Bringing Washburn's New Physical Anthropology into 2010 and Beyond—the 2008 AAPA Luncheon Lecture." *American Journal of Physical Anthropology* 143 (S51): 2–12.

———. 2012. *Race, Monogamy, and Other Lies They Told You: Busting Myths about Human Nature.* Berkeley: University of California Press.

———. 2014. "Human Evolution, Niche Complexity, and the Emergence of a Distinctively Human Imagination." *Time and Mind* 7 (3): 241–257. https://doi.org/10.1080/1751696X.2014.945720.

———. 2015. "Integrative Anthropology and the Human Niche: Toward a Contemporary Approach to Human Evolution." *American Anthropologist* 117 (2): 302–315. https://doi.org/10.1111/aman.12248.

Fuentes, Agustín, and Jeremy MacClancy, eds. 2013. *Ethics in the Field: Contemporary Challenges.* New York: Berghahn Books.

Gumert, Michael D., Agustín Fuentes, and Lisa Jones-Engel, eds. 2011. *Monkeys on the Edge: Ecology and Management of Long-Tailed Macaques and Their Interface with Humans.* Oxford: Oxford University Press.

AMY GOLDENBERG was the managing editor of *Anthropology News* from 2010 until 2015. She now works at the American Society of Cataract and Refractive Surgery, where she plans, manages, and coordinates the editorial activities of *EyeWorld*, a monthly newsmagazine. She graduated from Indiana University at Bloomington with a PhD in folklore. Her dissertation research was in Polish amber art.

MARY L. GRAY is a senior researcher at Microsoft Research and fellow at Harvard University's Berkman Klein Center for Internet and Society. She maintains a faculty position in the School of Informatics, Computing, and Engineering with affiliations in the Department of Anthropology, the Department of Gender Studies, and the Media School at Indiana University. Mary studies how technology access, material conditions, and everyday uses of media and technology transform people's lives. Her research has appeared in publications that include the *Harvard Business Review*, the *International Journal of Communication*, *Cultural Anthropology*, the *New York Times*, the *Los Angeles Times*, and *Forbes*. She served on the AAA's executive board and currently sits on the executive boards of the One Hundred Year Study on Artificial Intelligence and PRIM&R (Public Responsibility in Medicine and Research).

Selected Publications

Gray, Mary L. 2009. *Out in the Country: Youth, Media, and Queer Visibility in Rural America.* Intersections: Transdisciplinary Perspectives on Genders and Sexualities. New York: New York University Press.

———. 2015. "Resisting a Straight Narrative: The Politics of Visibility beyond (My) Identity Politics." Fieldsights: Theorizing the Contemporary, July 21, 2015. https://culanth.org/fieldsights/resisting-a-straight-narrative-the-politics-of-visibility-beyond-my-identity-politics.

———. 2018. "'There Are No Gay People Here': Expanding the Boundaries of Queer Youth Visibility in the Rural United States." In *Appalachia in Regional Context: Place Matters*, edited by Dwight B. Billings and Ann E. Kingsolver, 111–130. Lexington: University of Kentucky Press.

Gray, Mary L., and Siddharth Suri. 2019. *Ghost Work: How to Stop Silicon Valley from Building a New Global Underclass*. Boston: Houghton Mifflin Harcourt.

SARAH FRANCESCA GREEN is professor of social and cultural anthropology at the University of Helsinki. She is a specialist on borders, spatial relations, gender and sexuality, and information and communications technologies. She has lived in Greece, the United Kingdom, the United States, and Italy and currently lives in Helsinki, Finland.

She obtained her PhD in social anthropology at Cambridge University in 1992. She has held positions at the University of Cambridge; Manchester University, where she also served as the head of social anthropology (2007–2010); and other UK universities.

Sarah's major conceptual interest lies consistently in the notion of location; throughout her diverse fieldwork projects she has explored, in both literal and metaphorical senses, how people locate themselves in the world and in relation to themselves and others. For her, such locating practices are inextricably linked to political conditions, as well as social and epistemological elements. Her research themes include the politics of gender and sexuality in London; the politics of the intense promotion of information and communications technologies in Manchester; shifting perceptions of environment and land degradation in the Argolid valley and northwestern Greece; concepts of border relations on the Greek-Albanian border; the appearance, disappearance, and reappearance of the Balkans; the circulation of money in the Aegean; the notion of trust and the United Kingdom's new financial elites; and, since 2006, the shifting concept of border in the eastern peripheries of Europe.

Her book *Notes from the Balkans* (2005) won the William A. Douglass Prize in Europeanist Anthropology in 2006 and has been translated into Polish and Greek.

Selected Publications

Green, Sarah. 1997. *Urban Amazons: Lesbian Feminism and beyond in the Gender, Sexuality and Identity Battles of London*. London: Macmillan.
———. 2005. *Notes from the Balkans: Locating Marginality and Ambiguity on the Greek-Albanian Border*. Princeton, NJ: Princeton University Press.
Malm, Lena, and Sarah Green. 2013. *Borderwork: A Visual Journey through Periphery Frontier Regions*. Helsinki: Jasilti.

MONICA HELLER is a linguistic anthropologist and full professor at the University of Toronto's Ontario Institute for Studies in Education with a joint appointment to the Department of Anthropology. She is a member of the Royal Society of Canada. She was president of the AAA from 2013 to 2015. She is one of the few scholars at a non-U.S. institution to lead the AAA in the organization's history. She attended Swarthmore College in Pennsylvania, graduating with a bachelor of arts in sociology and anthropology (minor in linguistics) with honors in 1976. She earned her PhD in linguistics at the University of California, Berkeley, in 1982.

When Monica was growing up in Montreal, Canada, her father was a neurologist and her mother a medical sociologist. The political meanings of the uses of French and English in Quebec in the 1960s led to her interest in language and its influence on society. Her research has focused on the role of language in the construction of social difference and social inequality, especially francophone Canada, and she has also done comparative work in Western Europe. Using a political economy approach, she has tracked shifts in ideologies of language, nation, and state and examined processes of linguistic commodification in the globalized economy, along with the emergence of postnational ideologies of language and identity.

Heller has been a visiting professor at universities in Brazil, Belgium, Germany, France, Spain, and Finland and a fellow of the Freiburg Institute for Advanced Studies at the Albert-Ludwigs-Universität Freiburg in Germany. She also has an appointment in the Département d'études françaises at the Université de Moncton. From 2007 to 2012, she served as associate editor for the *Journal of Sociolinguistics*.

Selected Publications

Duchêne, Alexandre and Monica Heller, eds. 2007. *Discourses of Endangerment: Ideology and Interest in the Defense of Languages*. London: Continuum.
———, eds. 2012. *Language in Late Capitalism: Pride and Profit*. London: Routledge.
Heller, Monica. 1994. *Crosswords: Language, Ethnicity and Education in French Ontario*. Berlin: Mouton de Gruyter.
———. 1999. *Linguistic Minorities and Modernity: A Sociolinguistic Ethnography*. 2nd ed. London: Longman.
———. 2002. *Éléments d'une sociolinguistique critique*. Paris: Didier.
———, ed. 2007. *Bilingualism: A Social Approach*. London: Palgrave Macmillan.
———. 2010. "The Commodification of Language." *Annual Review of Anthropology* 39:101–114.
———. 2011. *Paths to Postnationalism: A Critical Ethnography of Language and Identity*. Oxford: Oxford University Press.
Heller, Monica, Lindsay Bell, Michelle Daveluy, Mireille McLaughlin, and Hubert Noël. 2015. *Sustaining the Nation: The Making and Moving of Language and Nation*. Oxford: Oxford University Press.
Heller, Monica, and Normand Labrie, eds. 2003. *Discours et identités: La francité canadienne entre modernité et mondialisation*. Cortil-Wodon, Belgium: Editions modulaires européennes: InterCommunications.

DOUGLAS HERTZLER is a senior policy analyst at ActionAid USA. Since 2012 his work has focused on Indigenous and community land rights and food sovereignty. He advocates for the fulfillment of human rights in agricultural and land policies of governments and institutions such as the World Bank and the United Nations.

Doug received a PhD in anthropology from the University of Iowa in 2002, and he has conducted research on social movements and land rights in Bolivia. Before that, he spent over five years living in Indigenous peasant villages in eastern Bolivia, where he worked on agroforestry and other community projects.

From 2001 through 2012, he served as a faculty member at Eastern Mennonite University and as associate director of the Washington Community Scholars' Center, where he engaged students in issues of urban social justice.

Doug has a personal background in agriculture, having been raised in dairy, corn, soy, and vegetable farming in central Pennsylvania.

Selected Publications

Hertzler, Douglas. 2005. "Campesinos and Originarios! Class and Ethnicity in Rural Movements in the Bolivian Lowlands." *Journal of Latin American Anthropology* 10 (1): 45–71.

———. 2015. "The New Alliance Model Doesn't Work: More Evidence from Tanzania." ActionAid USA, July 2, 2015. https://www.actionaidusa.org/blog/the-new -alliance-model-doesnt-work-more-evidence-from-tanzania/.

———. 2017. *Land Rights, Palm Oil and Conflict in Guatemala*. Washington, DC: ActionAid USA.

———. 2017. *Soybean Plantations: A Threat to Communities in the Cerrado Amazon Transition Zone*. Washington, DC: ActionAid USA.

Hertzler, Douglas, and Kathryn Ledebur. 2007. "Bolivia's Land Reform Legislation." Andean Information Network, January 2007.

EDWARD LIEBOW became executive director of the AAA in 2013. As executive director, Ed is responsible for promoting global scholarly exchange through research conferences and a publication portfolio with twenty-two titles. The association is also the public face of anthropology, and Ed is dedicated to highlighting the remarkable contributions that anthropologists make to serving the public interest. Before joining the association staff, Ed had a long career with the Battelle Memorial Institute, the world's largest not-for-profit research and development organization. Ed first joined Battelle in 1986, the year he received his PhD in cultural anthropology from Arizona State University. He has conducted research and public policy analysis on a variety of energy, public health, and social policy issues concerning disadvantaged communities. He maintains a position as affiliate associate professor of anthropology and interdisciplinary studies at the University of Washington. He has been a visiting professor of applied anthropology and comparative economics at Università Carlo Cattaneo Castellanza, Italy; has been a senior fellow of the Fulbright Commission; and has served on the faculty of the CDC-sponsored Summer Evaluation

Institute. He has also served on the executive boards of the AAA, the Society for Applied Anthropology, the Ethnographic Praxis in Industry Conference, and the Jack Straw Media Arts Foundation.

Selected Publications

Christenson, Robert H., Susan R. Snyder, Colleen S. Shaw, James H. Derzon, Robert S. Black, Diana Mass, Paul Epner, Alessandra M. Favoretto, and Edward B. Liebow. 2011. "Laboratory Medicine Best Practices: Systematic Evidence Review and Evaluation Methods for Quality Improvement." *Clinical Chemistry* 57 (6): 816–825. PMID: 21515742.

Liebow, Edward B. 2002. "Environmental Anthropology." In *The Handbook of Environmental Psychology: Environmental Psychology to Make a Difference*, edited by Robert B. Bechtel and Arza Churchman, 147–159. New York: Wiley and Sons.

———. 2007. "Public Health in an Era of Forced Federalism." In *Half-Lives and Half-Truths: Confronting the Radioactive Legacies of the Cold War*, edited by Barbara R. Johnston, 145–163. Santa Fe: School of American Research Press.

———. 2013. "On Evidence and the Public Interest." *American Anthropologist* 115 (4): 642–655. https://doi.org/10.1111/aman.12053.

Liebow, Edward B., Jerry Phelps, Bennett Van Houten, Shyanika Rose, Carlyn Orians, Jennifer Cohen, Philip Monroe, and Christina H. Drew. 2009. "Towards the Assessment of Scientific and Public Health Impacts of the NIEHS Extramural Asthma Research Program Using Available Data." *Environmental Health Perspectives* 117 (7): 1147–1154. PMC2717143.

MARIANO PERELMAN holds a PhD in social anthropology from the Universidad de Buenos Aires. He is a professor in the Doctoral Program in Social Sciences and professor of the Department of Anthropology at the Universidad de Buenos Aires. He is adjunct researcher at the Consejo Nacional de Investigaciones Científicas y Técnicas (Argentina) and researcher at the Urban Studies Area of the Instituto Gino Germini. His research focuses on informal work in public space, the formation of social inequalities, economic anthropology, and the anthropology of informal work. He has published several articles and book chapters. He has recently edited *Desigualdades persistentes y territorialidades emergentes: Disputas por el espacio urbano* (2018; with Mercedes Di Virgilio); *Fronteras en la ciudad: (Re)producción de desigualdades y conflictos urbanos* (2017; with Martín Boy); and *Disputas em torno do Espaço Público Urbano: Processos de Produção/Construção e Apropriação das cidades* (2017; with John Gledhill and Mariela Gabriela Hita).

Selected Publications

Perelman, Mariano. 2015. "Viejos y nuevos cirujas: Construcciones temporales y espaciales en la Ciudad de Buenos Aires" [Old and new *cirujas*: Temporo-spatial constructions in the city of Buenos Aires]. *Cuadernos de Antropología Social* 42:125–141.

———. 2017. "Vender nos ônibus: Os Buscas na cidade de Buenos Aires, Argentina" [Sell on buses: The *Buscas* in the city of Buenos Aires, Argentina]. *Tempo Social* 29 (1): 69–87.

———. 2019. "Inequality and Marginalization: Argentinean Urban Precarity." In *Routledge Handbook of Anthropology and the City: Engaging the Urban and the Future*, edited by Setha Low, 17–30. London: Routledge.

JEREMY "JERRY" ARAC SABLOFF is an American anthropologist. He is external professor and past president of the Santa Fe Institute in New Mexico and Christopher H. Browne Distinguished Professor of Anthropology, Emeritus, at the University of Pennsylvania. Jeremy is an expert on ancient Maya civilization and preindustrial urbanism. His academic interests have included settlement pattern studies, archaeological theory and method, the history of archaeology, the relevance of archaeology in the modern world, complexity theory, and transdisciplinary science.

Jeremy received his bachelor's degree from the University of Pennsylvania and his PhD in 1969 from Harvard. Before the Santa Fe Institute, he taught at Harvard University, the University of Utah, the University of New Mexico, the University of Pittsburgh, and the University of Pennsylvania (where he also served as Williams Director of the University of Pennsylvania Museum from 1994 to 2004).

Jeremy is an outspoken proponent of science communication. In 2010 he delivered the distinguished lecture at the AAA's annual meeting, encouraging anthropologists to make their work accessible to their relevant publics and cultivate a new generation of scientist-communicators.

Jeremy is a member of the National Academy of Sciences and the American Philosophical Society and a fellow of the American Academy of Arts and Sciences, the Society of Antiquaries of London, and the American Association for the Advancement of Science. He is a past president of the Society for American Archaeology, a past anthropology section chair of the American Association for the Advancement of Science, and past editor of *American Antiquity*.

Selected Publications

Sabloff, Jeremy A. 1975. *Excavations at Seibal: Ceramics*. Peabody Museum Memoirs 13. Cambridge, MA: Harvard University Press.

———. (1989) 1997. *The Cities of Ancient Mexico*. Rev. ed. New York: Thames and Hudson.

———. (1990) 1994. *The New Archaeology and the Ancient Maya*. New pbk. ed. New York: W. H. Freeman.

———. 2008. *Archaeology Matters: Action Archaeology in the Modern World*. London: Routledge.

Willey, Gordon R., and Jeremy A. Sabloff. (1974) 1993. *A History of American Archaeology*. 3rd ed. New York: W. H. Freeman.

CAROLYN SARGENT is professor of sociocultural anthropology and women, gender, and sexuality studies at Washington University in Saint Louis, Missouri. She earned her master's at the University of Manchester in 1970 and her PhD at Michigan State University in 1979.

Carolyn's research and teaching are primarily situated in the domain of gender and health, with a particular focus on reproduction, medical decision making, and the management of women's health in low-income populations. Her main teaching and research interests center on translation as illness experience, the social course of illness, the transnational production of community, immigration and health, the anthropology of cancer, and the politics of reproduction.

She has worked in West Africa (Benin, Mali) and Jamaica, and her research in progress involves West African and North African immigrants living with breast cancer in France, and the collective production of meanings and strategies about this condition.

Carolyn is past president of the Society for Medical Anthropology. She created the SMA National Health Task Force because she felt that medical anthropologists could give valuable information and perspectives on the national health-care debate. She intended to develop the concept of "research on demand." This would involve offering anthropologists' research efforts to legislators who were planning on making a policy change. She encourages anthropologists to work toward shaping public discourse and policy. To this end, she served as a community representative to two hospital ethics committees while she lived in Dallas, Texas, and is currently a member of the Barnes Jewish Hospital ethics committee in Saint Louis.

Selected Publications

Brettell, Caroline B., and Carolyn F. Sargent, eds. 2016. *Gender in Cross-Cultural Perspective.* 7th ed., rev. Englewood Cliffs, NJ: Prentice-Hall.

Sargent, Carolyn F. 2006. "Reproductive Strategies and Islamic Discourse: Malian Migrants Negotiate Everyday Life in Paris, France." In "Medical Anthropology in the Muslim World." Special issue, *Medical Anthropology Quarterly* 20 (1): 31–50.

Sargent, Carolyn F., and Carole H. Browner, eds. 2011. *Globalization, Reproduction, and the State.* Durham, NC: Duke University Press.

Sargent, Carolyn, and Stephanie Larchanché. 2011. "Transnational Migration and Global Health: The Production and Management of Risk, Illness, and Access to Care." *Annual Review of Anthropology* 40:345–361.

Sargent, Carolyn, and Carolyn Smith-Morris. 2006. "Questioning Our Principles: Anthropological Contributions to Ethical Dilemmas in Clinical Practice." *Cambridge Quarterly of Healthcare Ethics* 15 (2): 123–134.

MARILYN STRATHERN is emeritus professor of social anthropology, University of Cambridge, and was, from 1998 to 2009, mistress of Girton College, Cambridge.

A presidential chair of the European Association of Social Anthropologists, former trustee of the National Museums and Galleries on Merseyside, and an honorary fellow of Trinity College, she was named Dame Commander of the British Empire in 2001 (the first such honor in the subject for nearly thirty years). She became (hon.) life president of the Association of Social Anthropologists of the UK and Commonwealth in 2008.

Marilyn's interests have been divided between Melanesian and British ethnography: Papua New Guinea has been a principal area of fieldwork from 1964 to most recently in 2015, although she is also intrigued by developments in knowledge practices in the United Kingdom and Europe. Melanesia is never far from her concerns; in 2009 the University of Papua New Guinea bestowed an honorary degree on her, following Copenhagen, Durham, Edinburgh, Oxford, and others. Initial work on gender relations led in two directions: feminist scholarship and the new reproductive technologies (1980s–1990s) and legal systems and intellectual and cultural property (1970s, 1990–2000s). She is best known for *The Gender of the Gift* (1988), a critique of anthropological theories of society and gender relations applied to Melanesia, which she paired with *After Nature: English Kinship in the Late Twentieth Century* (1992), a comment on the cultural revolution at home. Her most experimental work is an exercise on the comparative method called *Partial Connections* (1991). Over the last twenty years, she has published on reproductive technologies, intellectual and cultural property rights, and interdisciplinarity, although it is her brief work on regimes of audit and accountability that has attracted the most widespread attention recently. Some of these themes are brought together in *Kinship, Law and the Unexpected* (2005).

Selected Publications

Strathern, Marilyn. 1972. *Women in Between: Female Roles in a Male World: Mount Hagen, New Guinea*. Lanham, MD: Rowman and Littlefield.

———. 1988. *The Gender of the Gift: Problems with Women and Problems with Society in Melanesia*. Berkeley: University of California Press.

———. 1991. *Partial Connections*. Lanham, MD: AltaMira.

———. 1992. *After Nature: English Kinship in the Late Twentieth Century*. Cambridge: Cambridge University Press.

———. 2005. *Kinship, Law and the Unexpected: Relatives Are Always a Surprise*. Cambridge: Cambridge University Press.

NANDINI SUNDAR is professor of sociology at the Delhi School of Economics, Delhi University. Her publications include *Subalterns and Sovereigns: An Anthropological History of Bastar* (2nd ed. 2007; translated into Hindi as *Gunda Dhur Ki Talash Mein*, 2009); *Branching Out: Joint Forest Management in India* (2001; coauthored); and *The Burning Forest: India's War in Bastar* (2016). Her edited volumes include *The Scheduled Tribes and Their India* (2016); *Civil Wars in South Asia: State, Sovereignty, Development* (2014; coedited with Aparna Sundar); *Legal Grounds: Natural Resources, Identity and the Law in Jharkhand* (2009); *Anthropology in the East: The Founders of Indian Sociology and Anthropology* (2007, coedited); and *A New Moral Economy for India's Forests: Discourses of Community and Participation* (1999). She was editor of *Contributions to Indian Sociology* from 2007 to 2011 and serves on the boards of several journals.

In 2010, she was awarded the Infosys Prize in Social Sciences-Social Anthropology, and in 2016, the Ester Boserup Prize for Research on Development. Her public writings are available at http://nandinisundar.blogspot.com.

Selected Publications

Deshpande, Satish, Nandini Sundar, and Patricia Uberoi, eds. 2007. *Anthropology in the East: The Founders of Indian Sociology and Anthropology*. Delhi: Permanent Black.

Sundar, Nandini. (1997) 2007. *Subalterns and Sovereigns: An Anthropological History of Bastar*. 2nd ed. Oxford: Oxford University Press.

———. 2011. "The Rule of Law and Citizenship in Central India: Post-Colonial Dilemmas." *Citizenship Studies* 15 (3–4): 419–432.

———. 2014. "Mimetic Sovereignties, Precarious Citizenship: State Effects in a Looking Glass World." *Journal of Peasant Studies* 41 (4): 469–490.

Sundar, Nandini, and Aparna Sundar, eds. 2014. *Civil Wars in South Asia: State, Sovereignty, Development*. Los Angeles: Sage.

ALAKA WALI is curator of North American anthropology at Chicago's Field Museum. Her work explores and examines social contexts of human-ecological interactions, from urban settings to the Amazonian regions of Peru. Her projects have entailed community engagement and environmental conservation via arts programs in poor communities; the promotion of social, cultural, and artistic aspects of Mexican immigrant lifeways; and social cohesion using arts programs and arts-based strategies. Alaka has received major grants from the Ford Foundation, the National Endowment for the Humanities, the Rockefeller Foundation, the John D. and Catherine T. MacArthur Foundation, and the National Science Foundation. She has spoken at community organizations in Chicago and appeared on public radio and television programs. She is author of two books, several monographs, and over forty articles, and she is past editorial board member of *American Anthropologist*.

Selected Publications

Mullings, Leith, and Alaka Wali. 2001. *Stress and Resilience: The Social Context of Reproduction in Central Harlem*. New York: Kluwar Academic/Plenum.

Ostergaard, Josh, Madeleine Tudor, and Alaka Wali. 2006. *Collaborative Research: A*

Practical Introduction to Participatory Action Research for Communities and Scholars. Chicago: Field Museum. http://www.fieldmuseum.org.

Tudor, Madeleine, and Alaka Wali. 2015. "Showcasing Heritage: Engaging Local Communities through Museum Practice." In *Participatory Visual and Digital Research in Action*, edited by Aline Gubrium, Krista Harper, and Marty Otañez, 197–212. Walnut Creek, CA: Left Coast.

Wali, Alaka. 1989. *Kilowatts and Crisis: Hydroelectric Power and Social Dislocation in Eastern Panama*. Development, Conflict and Social Change. Boulder, CO: Westview.

———. 2015. "Listening with Passion: A Journey through Engagement and Exchange." In *Anthropology's Changing Terms of Engagement*, edited by Roger Sanjek, 174–190. Philadelphia: University of Pennsylvania Press.

Wali, Alaka, and J. Claire Odland, eds. 2016. *The Shipibo-Conibo: Cultures and Collections in Context*. Fieldiana Anthropology, n.s., 45. Chicago: Field Museum of Natural History.

Wali, Alaka, and Madeleine Tudor. 2015. "Crossing the Line: Participatory Action Research in a Museum Setting." In *Public Anthropology in a Borderless World*, edited by Sam Beck and Carl A. Maida, 66–88. New York: Berghahn.

References

Allen, Jafari Sinclaire, and Ryan Cecil Jobson. 2016. "The Decolonizing Generation (Race and) Theory in Anthropology since the Eighties." *Current Anthropology* 57 (2): 129–148.

Archeological Institute of America. n.d. "Pomerance Award for Scientific Contributions to Archaeology." Accessed September 26, 2019. https://www.archaeological .org/grant/pomerance-award-for-scientific-contributions/.

Bennett, Linda, T. J. Ferguson, J. Anthony Paredes, Susan Squires, Judy Tso, and Dennis Wiedman. 2006. *Final Report: Practicing Advisory Work Group (PAWG)*. American Anthropological Association. http://www.americananthro.org /ParticipateAndAdvocate/Content.aspx?ItemNumber=2020.

Biehl, João. 2005. *Vita: Life in a Zone of Social Abandonment*. Berkeley: University of California Press.

———. 2007. *Will to Live: AIDS Therapies and the Politics of Survival*. Princeton, NJ: Princeton University Press.

Blommaert, Jan. 2009. "Language, Asylum, and the National Order." *Current Anthropology* 50 (4): 415–441.

Boas, Franz. 1906. *The Measurement of Differences between Variable Quantities*. New York: Science Press.

———. 1911. *The Mind of Primitive Man*. New York: Macmillan.

———. 1927. *Primitive Art*. Oslo: H. Aschhoug.

———. 1945. *Race and Democratic Society*. New York: Augustin.

———. 1966. *Kwakiutl Ethnography*. Edited by Helen Codere. Chicago: University of Chicago Press.

Bourgois, Philippe. 2001. "The Power of Violence in War and Peace: Post-Cold War Lessons from El Salvador." *Ethnography* 2 (1): 5–34.

Briggs, Charles L. 2007. "Mediating Infanticide: Theorizing Relations between Narrative and Violence." *Cultural Anthropology* 22 (3): 315–356.

Brondo, Keri Vacanti, and Linda A. Bennett. 2012. "Career Subjectivities in US Anthropology: Gender, Practice, and Resistance." *American Anthropologist* 114 (4): 598–610.

Brondo, Keri Vacante, Linda Bennett, Harmony Farner, Cindy Martin, and Andrew Mrkva. 2009. *Work Climate, Gender, and the Status of Practicing Anthropologists:*

Report Commissioned by the Committee on the Status of Women in Anthropology. Prepared for the American Anthropological Association. http://s3.amazonaws .com/rdcms-aaa/files/production/public/FileDownloads/pdfs/resources /departments/upload/COSWA-REPORT-ON-PRACTICING -ANTHROPOLOGY-2.pdf.

Cabrera, Lydia. 1954. *El monte: Igbo finda, ewe orisha, vititi nfinda (Notas sobre las religiones, la magia, las supersticiones y el folklore de los negros criollos y del pueblo de Cuba).* Havana: Ediciones C. R.

Campbell, Bernard. 1966. *Human Evolution: An Introduction to Man's Adaptations.* Chicago: Aldine.

Chomsky, Noam. 2014. *The Quotable Chomsky.* Roodepoort, South Africa: Rodney Ulyate.

———. 2015. *What Kind of Creatures Are We?* New York: Columbia University Press.

Chomsky, Noam, and Michel Foucault. 2006. *The Chomsky-Foucault Debate: On Human Nature.* New York: New Press, distributed by W. W. Norton.

Davis, Shelton H. 1977. *Victims of the Miracle: Development and the Indians of Brazil.* Cambridge: Cambridge University Press.

———. 1988. *Land Rights and Indigenous Peoples: The Role of the Inter-American Commission on Human Rights.* Cambridge, MA: Cultural Survival.

———, ed. 1993. *Indigenous Views of Land and the Environment.* World Bank Discussion Papers No. 188. Washington, DC: World Bank. http://documents .worldbank.org/curated/en/720271468741314548/Indigenous-views-of-land-and -the-environment.

Davis, Shelton H., and Katrinka Ebbe, eds. 1995. *Traditional Knowledge and Sustainable Development.* Environmentally Sustainable Development Proceedings Series No. 4. Washington, DC: World Bank. http://documents.worldbank.org/curated /en/517861468766175944/Traditional-knowledge-and-sustainable-development.

Dolhinow, Phyllis, ed. 1972. *Primate Patterns.* New York: Holt, Rinehart and Winston.

———. *See also* Jay, Phyllis C.

Dolhinow, Phyllis, and Vincent Sarich. 1971. *Background for Man: Readings in Physical Anthropology.* Boston: Little, Brown.

Dominguez, Virginia R. 2012. "Comfort Zones and Their Dangers: Who Are We? *Qui Sommes-Nous?*" *American Anthropologist* 114 (3): 394–405.

———, ed. 2018. "Walls, Material and Rhetorical: Past, Present, and Future." Special issue, *Review of International American Studies* 11 (1).

Dominguez, Virginia R., and Emily Metzner. 2017. "Foreword: Special Section on Nativism, Nationalism, and Xenophobia: What Anthropologists Do and Have Done." *American Anthropologist* 119 (3): 518–519.

Dunn, Cynthia D. 2014. "Then I Learned about Positive Thinking: The Genre Structuring of Narratives of Self-Transformation." *Journal of Linguistic Anthropology* 24 (2): 133–150.

Durkheim, Emile. 1893. *The Division of Labour in Society.* [In French.] Paris: Presses Universitaires de France.

———. 1895. *The Rules of the Sociological Method.* [In French.] Paris: Librairie Felix Alcan.

———. 1897. *Suicide: A Study in Sociology.* [In French.] Paris: Librairie Felix Alcan.

———. 1912. *Elementary Forms of the Religious Life.* London: George Allen and Unwin.

Eiseley, Loren. 1957. *The Immense Journey*. New York: Vintage Books, Random House.

———. 1958. *Darwin's Century*. New York: Doubleday.

———. 1969. *The Unexpected Universe*. New York: Harcourt, Brace, and World.

———. 1971. *The Night Country: Reflections of a Bone-Hunting Man*. New York: Scribner.

———. 1975. *All the Strange Hours: The Excavation of a Life*. New York: Scribner.

Ellick, Carol, and Joe Watkins. 2011. *The Anthropology Graduate's Guide: From Student to a Career*. New York: Routledge.

Engelke, Matthew. 2018. *How to Think like an Anthropologist*. Princeton, NJ: Princeton University Press.

Evans-Pritchard, E. E. 1937. *Witchcraft, Oracles and Magic among the Azande*. Oxford: Oxford University Press.

———. 1940. *The Nuer: A Description of the Modes of Livelihood and Political Institutions of a Nilotic People*. Oxford: Clarendon.

———. 1949. *The Sanusi of Cyrenaica*. Oxford: Oxford University Press.

———. 1951. *Kinship and Marriage among the Nuer*. Oxford: Clarendon.

———. 1956. *Nuer Religion*. Oxford: Clarendon.

———. 1962. *Social Anthropology and Other Essays*. New York: Free Press.

———. 1965. *Theories of Primitive Religion*. Oxford: Oxford University Press.

Feldman-Bianco, Bela, and Miguel Vale de Almeida. 2018. "Interview: World Anthropologies: A Portuguese-Brazilian Conversation." *American Anthropologist* 120 (1): 126–137.

Field, Les, and Richard Fox, eds. 2007. *Anthropology Put to Work*. Oxford: Berg.

Fortes, Meyer. 1945. *The Dynamics of Clanship among the Tallensi*. Oxford: Oxford University Press.

———. 1949. *The Web of Kinship among the Tallensi*. Oxford: Oxford University Press.

———. 1958. *Oedipus and Job in West African Religion*. Cambridge: Cambridge University Press.

———. 1970. *Time and Social Structure and Other Essays*. London: University of London, Athlone Press.

Fortes, Meyer, and E. E. Evans-Pritchard, eds. 1940. *African Political Systems*. London: International African Institute.

French, Brigittine. 2015. "Narratives of Violence in 'Post-Conflict' Guatemala: Impunity and the Transnational Politics of Misrecognition." In *The Performance of Memory As Transitional Justice*, edited by Elizabeth Bird and Fraser Ottanelli, 153–166. Antwerp: Intersentia Publishers.

Geertz, Clifford. 1973. *The Interpretation of Cultures*. New York: Basic Books.

———. 1988. *Works and Lives: The Anthropologist as Author*. Stanford, CA: Stanford University Press.

———. 1995. *After the Fact: Two Countries, Four Decades, One Anthropologist*. Cambridge, MA: Harvard University Press.

Gill, Lesley. 1987. *Peasants, Entrepreneurs, and Social Change*. Boulder, CO: Westview.

Gluckman, Max. 1954. *Rituals of Rebellion in South-East Africa*. Manchester: Manchester University Press.

———. 1963. *Order and Rebellion in Tribal Africa*. London: Cohen and West.

———. 1965. *Politics, Law and Ritual in Tribal Society*. Chicago: Aldine.

———. 1972. *The Allocation of Responsibility*. Manchester: Manchester University Press.

Goffman, Erving. 1959. *The Presentation of Self in Everyday Life*. Garden City, NY: Doubleday.

Goodwin, Charles. 1994. "Professional Vision." *American Anthropologist* 96 (3): 606–633.

Haviland, John B. 2003. "Ideologies of Language: Some Reflections on Language and U.S. Law." *American Anthropologist* 105 (4): 764–774.

Herzfeld, Michael. 2001. *Anthropology: Theoretical Practice in Culture and Society*. Malden, MA: Blackwell.

Hirschman, Albert. 1971. *A Bias for Hope: Essays on Development and Latin America*. New Haven, CT: Yale University Press.

———. 1977. *The Passions and the Interests: Political Arguments for Capitalism before Its Triumph*. Princeton, NJ: Princeton University Press.

———. 1981. *Essays in Trespassing: Economics to Politics and Beyond*. New York: Cambridge University Press.

———. 1984. *Getting Ahead Collectively: Grassroots Experiences in Latin America*. With photographs by Mitchell Denburg. New York: Pergamon.

———. 1991. *The Rhetoric of Reaction: Perversity, Futility, Jeopardy*. Cambridge, MA: Belknap Press of Harvard University Press.

———. 1995. *A Propensity to Self-Subversion*. Cambridge, MA: Harvard University Press.

InformIT. n.d. "Bernard G. Campbell." Pearson. Accessed September 26, 2019. http://www.informit.com/authors/bio/e2307abd-652a-4029-bc4d-f188c941a3d1.

Jay, Phyllis C., ed. 1968. *Primates: Studies in Adaptation and Variability*. New York: Holt, Rinehart and Winston.

———. *See also* Dolhinow, Phyllis.

Kramer, Samuel N. 1988. *In the World of Sumer*. Detroit: Wayne State University Press.

Lakoff, George. 1996. *Moral Politics: What Conservatives Know That Liberals Don't*. Chicago: University of Chicago Press.

Lakoff, George, and Mark Johnson. 1980. *Metaphors We Live By*. Chicago: University of Chicago Press.

Larsen, Helge, and Froelich Rainey. 1948. *Ipiutak and the Arctic Whale Hunting Culture*. Anthropological Papers of the American Museum of Natural History, vol. 42. New York: American Museum of Natural History.

Leach, Edmund. 1954. *Political Systems of Highland Burma: A Study of Kachin Social Structure*. Cambridge, MA: Harvard University Press.

———. 1961. *Pul Eliya: A Village in Ceylon*. Cambridge: Cambridge University Press.

Leap, William L., and Tom Boellstorff, eds. 2004. *Speaking in Queer Tongues: Globalization and Gay Language*. Urbana: University of Illinois Press.

Levi-Strauss, Claude. 1955. *Tristes tropiques*. Paris: Librairie Plon.

———. 1962. *La pensee sauvage* [The savage mind]. Paris: Librairie Plon.

———. 1963. *Structural Anthropology*. Translated by Claire Jacobson and Brooke Grundfest Schoepf. New York: Doubleday Anchor Books.

Marks, Jonathan. 2009. *Why I Am Not a Scientist: Anthropology and Modern Knowledge*. Berkeley: University of California Press.

Marx, Karl. (1867) 2004. *Capital*. London: Penguin Books.

———. (1939) 1973. *Grundrisse: Foundations of the Critique of Political Economy*. London: Penguin Books in association with New Left Review.

———. (1961) 2007. *The Economic and Philosophic Manuscripts of 1844*. Mineola, NY: Dover.

Marx, Karl, and Friedrich Engels. (1848) 1906. *The Communist Manifesto*. Chicago: Charles H. Kerr.

Melton, Gary B., and Laura Nader. 1986. *The Law as a Behavioral Instrument*. Lincoln: University of Nebraska Press.

Mintz, Sidney W. (1960) 1974. *Worker in the Cane: A Puerto Rican Life History*. New York: W. W. Norton.

———. 1974. *Caribbean Transformations*. Baltimore: Johns Hopkins University Press.

———. 1986. *Sweetness and Power: The Place of Sugar in Modern History*. London: Penguin Books.

———. 1996. *Tasting Food, Tasting Freedom: Excursions into Eating, Culture, and the Past*. Boston: Beacon.

Morgan, Lewis Henry. 1871. *Systems of Consanguinity and Affinity of the Human Family*. Washington, DC: Smithsonian Institution.

———. 1877. *Ancient Society*. Chicago: Charles Kerr.

Mullings, Leith. 2015. "Anthropology Matters." *American Anthropologist* 117 (1): 4–16.

Nader, Laura. 1964. *Talea and Juquila: A Comparison of Zapotec Social Organization*. Berkeley: University of California Press.

———. 1965. *The Ethnography of Law*. Menasha, WI: American Anthropological Association.

———, dir. 1966. *To Make the Balance*. Berkeley: University of California Extension Media Center. Film, 33 min.

———, 1980. *Little Injustices: Laura Nader Looks at the Law*. Washington, DC: Film Broadcasting Associates. Film, 60 min.

———. 1981. *No Access to Law: Alternatives to the American Judicial System*. New York: Academic Press.

———. 1990. *Harmony Ideology: Justice and Control in a Zapotec Mountain Village*. Stanford, CA: Stanford University Press.

———. 1996. *Naked Science: Anthropological Inquiry into Boundaries, Power, and Knowledge*. New York: Routledge.

———. 2002. *The Life of the Law: Anthropological Projects*. Berkeley: University of California Press.

———. 2010. *The Energy Reader*. Malden, MA: Wiley-Blackwell.

———, dir. 2011. *Losing Knowledge: Fifty Years of Change*. Berkeley: Berkeley Media. Film, 40 min.

———. 2012. *Culture and Dignity: Dialogues between the Middle East and the West*. Malden, MA: Wiley-Blackwell.

———. 2015. *What the Rest Think of the West: Since 600 A.D.* Berkeley: University of California Press.

———. 2018. *Contrarian Anthropology: The Unwritten Rules of Academia*. New York: Berghahn Books.

Nader, Laura, and Harry F. Todd. 1978. *The Disputing Process: Law in Ten Societies*. New York: Columbia University Press.

Nardi, Bonnie, Celia Pearce, T. L. Taylor, and Tom Boellstorff. 2012. *Ethnography and Virtual Worlds: A Handbook of Method*. Princeton, NJ: Princeton University Press.

Ortiz, Fernando. 1906. *Los negros brujos*. Havana: Cubanas Ediciones.

———. 1916. *Los negros esclavos*. Havana: Cubanas Ediciones.

———. (1940) 1995. *Cuban Counterpoint: Tobacco and Sugar.* Translated by Harriet de Onís. Durham, NC: Duke University Press. Originally published as *Contrapunteo cubano del tabaco y el azúcar.*

———. (1950) 1998. *La Africania de la musica folklorica de Cuba.* Reprint, Madrid: Editorial Musica Mundana.

Oswalt, Wendell. 1966. *This Land Was Theirs: A Study of the North American Indian.* New York: Wiley.

———. 1972. *Habitat and Technology: The Evolution of Hunting.* New York: Holt, Rinehart and Winston.

———. 2012. *Bashful No Longer: Alaskan Eskimo Ethnohistory, 1778–1988.* Norman: University of Oklahoma Press.

———. n.d. "Professional Life." Wendell Oswalt's website. Accessed September 26, 2019. https://sites.google.com/site/wendelloswalt/about-anita/professional-life.

Petryna, Adriana. 2002. *Life Exposed: Biological Citizens after Chernobyl.* Princeton, NJ: Princeton University Press.

———. 2009. *When Experiments Travel: Clinical Trials and the Global Search for Human Subjects.* Princeton, NJ: Princeton University Press.

Putnam, Frederic. 1899. "A Problem in American Anthropology." *Science* 10 (243): 225–236.

Rabinow, Paul. 1975. *Symbolic Domination: Cultural Form and Historical Change in Morocco.* Chicago: University of Chicago Press.

———. 1977. *Reflections on Fieldwork in Morocco.* Berkeley: University of California Press.

———, ed. 1984. *The Foucault Reader.* New York: Pantheon Books.

———. 1989. *French Modern: Norms and Forms of the Social Environment.* Cambridge, MA: MIT Press.

———. 1996. *Making PCR: A Story of Biotechnology.* Chicago: University of Chicago Press.

———. 1997. *Essays on the Anthropology of Reason.* Princeton, NJ: Princeton University Press.

———. 1999. *French DNA: Trouble in Purgatory.* Chicago: University of Chicago Press.

———. 2003. *Anthropos Today: Reflections on Modern Equipment.* Princeton, NJ: Princeton University Press.

———. 2007. *Marking Time: On the Anthropology of the Contemporary.* Princeton, NJ: Princeton University Press.

———. 2011. *The Accompaniment: Assembling the Contemporary.* Chicago: University of Chicago Press.

Rabinow, Paul, and Hubert Dreyfus. 1983. *Michel Foucault: Beyond Structuralism and Hermeneutics.* Chicago: University of Chicago Press.

Rabinow, Paul, and Anthony Stavriankis. 2013. *Demands of the Day: On the Logic of Anthropological Inquiry.* Chicago: University of Chicago Press.

———. 2014. *Designs on the Contemporary: Anthropological Tests.* Chicago: University of Chicago Press.

Rabinow, Paul, and William Sullivan, eds. 1977. *Interpretive Social Science: A Reader.* Berkeley: University of California Press.

Radcliffe-Brown, A. R. 1922. *The Andaman Islanders: A Study in Social Anthropology.* Cambridge: Cambridge University Press.

———. 1952. *Structure and Function in Primitive Societies.* London: Cohen and West.

Rainey, Froelich. 1947. *The Whale Hunters of Tigara*. Anthropological Papers of the American Museum of Natural History, vol. 41, pt. 2. New York: American Museum of Natural History.

———. 1992. *Reflections of a Digger: Fifty Years of World Archaeology*. Philadelphia: University Museum of Archaeology and Anthropology, University of Pennsylvania.

Riesman, Paul. 1977. *Freedom in Fulani Social Life*. Chicago: University of Chicago Press.

Rousseau, Jean-Jacques. 1762. *The Social Contract, or Principles of Political Right (Du contrat social)*. Amsterdam: Chez Marc Michel Rey.

Sabloff, Jeremy A. 2011. "Where Have You Gone, Margaret Mead? Anthropology and Public Intellectuals." *American Anthropologist* 113 (3): 408–416.

Schwieder, Dorothy. Dorothy Schwieder (1933–2014), Papers, 1880–2011. Parks Library of Iowa State University.

Simic, Andrei. 1969. "Management of the Male Image in Yugoslavia." *Anthropological Quarterly* 42 (2): 89–101.

———. 1983. "Machismo and Cryptomatriarchy: Power, Affect, and Authority in the Contemporary Yugoslav Family." *Ethos* 11 (1–2): 66–86.

Sontag, Susan. 1977. *On Photography*. New York: Farrar, Straus and Giroux.

———. 2003. *Regarding the Pain of Others*. New York: Farrar, Straus and Giroux.

Strang, Veronica. 2009. *What Anthropologists Do*. Oxford: Berg/Bloomsbury.

Sweetser, Eve. 1990. *From Etymology to Pragmatics: Metaphorical and Cultural Aspects of Semantic Structure*. Cambridge: Cambridge University Press.

Todd, Zoe. 2018. "Decolonial Turn 2.0: The Reckoning." Anthrodendum, June 15, 2008. https://anthrodendum.org/2018/06/15/the-decolonial-turn-2-0-the-reckoning/.

Vogt, Evon. 1969. *Zinacantan: A Maya Community in the Highlands of Chiapas*. Cambridge, MA: Harvard University Press.

———. 1976. *Tortillas for the Gods: A Symbolic Analysis of Zinacanteco Rituals*. Cambridge, MA: Harvard University Press.

Wade, Nicholas. 2001. "Joseph Greenberg, 85, Singular Linguist, Dies." *New York Times*, May 15. https://www.nytimes.com/2001/05/15/us/joseph-greenberg-85-singular-linguist-dies.html.

Weber, Max. (1904–1905) 1930. *The Protestant Ethic and the Spirit of Capitalism*. Translated by Talcott Parsons. London: George Allen and Unwin. Originally published as *Die protestantische Ethik und der Geist des Kapitalismus*.

———. 1922. *Wirtschaft und Gesellschaft* [Economy and society]. Published posthumously by his widow, Marianne. Tubingen: Mohr.

———. 1946. *From Max Weber: Essays in Sociology*. Translated and edited by H. H. Gerth and C. Wright Mills. New York: Oxford University Press.

Whiteford, Michael, and John Friedl. 1991. *The Human Portrait: Introduction to Cultural Anthropology*. 3rd ed. Upper Saddle River, NJ: Prentice Hall.

Whiteford, Michael, and Scott Whiteford, eds. 1998. *Crossing Currents: Continuity and Change in Latin America*. Upper Saddle River, NJ: Prentice Hall.

Wikipedia. 2019a. "Fernando Ortiz Fernández." Last modified September 4, 2019. https://en.wikipedia.org/wiki/Fernando_Ortiz_Fern%C3%A1ndez.

———. 2019b. "Lydia Cabrera." Last modified September 4, 2019. https://en.wikipedia.org/wiki/Lydia_Cabrera.

———. 2019c. "Marshall Scholarship." Last modified November 7, 2019. https://en.wikipedia.org/wiki/Marshall_Scholarship.

Wolf, Eric. 1969. *Peasant Wars of the Twentieth Century*. New York: Harper and Row.
———. 1982. *Europe and the People without History*. Berkeley: University of California Press.
Wragg Sykes, Rebecca. n.d. "Sally Binford: Paradigm Shifter." TrowelBlazers. Accessed September 26, 2019. https://trowelblazers.com/sally-binford-paradigm -shifter/.

Index

Page numbers in italics indicate a photo.

About the Authors

VIRGINIA R. DOMINGUEZ is Gutgsell Professor at the University of Illinois at Urbana-Champaign, where she also is cofounder and consulting director of the International Forum for U.S. Studies. A former president of the American Anthropological Association, she is also the author, coauthor, editor, or coeditor of multiple books, most recently *America Observed* (with Jasmin Habib) and *Global Perspectives on the United States* (with Jane C. Desmond).

BRIGITTINE M. FRENCH is professor of anthropology at Grinnell College. She is a linguistic anthropologist whose work focuses on testimonial discourse, violence, gender, and rights in postconflict nations. She is the author of *Maya Ethnolinguistic Identity* and *Narratives of Conflict, Belonging, and the State: Discourse and Social Life in Post-War Ireland*.